T0344741

THIS IS YOUR **PASSBOOK®** FOR ...

REVENUE EQUIPMENT MAINTAINER

NATIONAL LEARNING CORPORATION®
passbooks.com

PASSBOOK® SERIES

THE *PASSBOOK® SERIES* has been created to prepare applicants and candidates for the ultimate academic battlefield – the examination room.

At some time in our lives, each and every one of us may be required to take an examination – for validation, matriculation, admission, qualification, registration, certification, or licensure.

Based on the assumption that every applicant or candidate has met the basic formal educational standards, has taken the required number of courses, and read the necessary texts, the *PASSBOOK® SERIES* furnishes the one special preparation which may assure passing with confidence, instead of failing with insecurity. Examination questions – together with answers – are furnished as the basic vehicle for study so that the mysteries of the examination and its compounding difficulties may be eliminated or diminished by a sure method.

This book is meant to help you pass your examination provided that you qualify and are serious in your objective.

The entire field is reviewed through the huge store of content information which is succinctly presented through a provocative and challenging approach – the question-and-answer method.

A climate of success is established by furnishing the correct answers at the end of each test.

You soon learn to recognize types of questions, forms of questions, and patterns of questioning. You may even begin to anticipate expected outcomes.

You perceive that many questions are repeated or adapted so that you can gain acute insights, which may enable you to score many sure points.

You learn how to confront new questions, or types of questions, and to attack them confidently and work out the correct answers.

You note objectives and emphases, and recognize pitfalls and dangers, so that you may make positive educational adjustments.

Moreover, you are kept fully informed in relation to new concepts, methods, practices, and directions in the field.

You discover that you arre actually taking the examination all the time: you are preparing for the examination by "taking" an examination, not by reading extraneous and/or supererogatory textbooks.

In short, this PASSBOOK®, used directedly, should be an important factor in helping you to pass your test.

REVENUE EQUIPMENT MAINTAINER

DUTIES

Revenue Equipment Maintainers test, diagnose, repair and perform preventive maintenance on bus and subway Automated Fare Collection equipment including, but not limited to, turnstiles, booth terminal equipment, MetroCard vending machines and bus fare boxes; diagnose, troubleshoot, remove and replace electronic circuit boards, wiring harnesses, electronic and electromechanical modular units and other components using digital multimeters, wiring schematics, palmtop computers and other special test equipment; and perform related work.

SCOPE OF THE EXAMINATION

The multiple-choice test may include questions on: electronic and electrical theory; the maintenance, troubleshooting and repair of electronic, electrical and mechanical equipment, including the selection and use of required tools and testing devices; reading and interpreting schematics; safe work practices, including first-aid procedures; and other related matters.

HOW TO TAKE A TEST

I. YOU MUST PASS AN EXAMINATION

A. *WHAT EVERY CANDIDATE SHOULD KNOW*

Examination applicants often ask us for help in preparing for the written test. What can I study in advance? What kinds of questions will be asked? How will the test be given? How will the papers be graded?

As an applicant for a civil service examination, you may be wondering about some of these things. Our purpose here is to suggest effective methods of advance study and to describe civil service examinations.

Your chances for success on this examination can be increased if you know how to prepare. Those "pre-examination jitters" can be reduced if you know what to expect. You can even experience an adventure in good citizenship if you know why civil service exams are given.

B. *WHY ARE CIVIL SERVICE EXAMINATIONS GIVEN?*

Civil service examinations are important to you in two ways. As a citizen, you want public jobs filled by employees who know how to do their work. As a job seeker, you want a fair chance to compete for that job on an equal footing with other candidates. The best-known means of accomplishing this two-fold goal is the competitive examination.

Exams are widely publicized throughout the nation. They may be administered for jobs in federal, state, city, municipal, town or village governments or agencies.

Any citizen may apply, with some limitations, such as the age or residence of applicants. Your experience and education may be reviewed to see whether you meet the requirements for the particular examination. When these requirements exist, they are reasonable and applied consistently to all applicants. Thus, a competitive examination may cause you some uneasiness now, but it is your privilege and safeguard.

C. *HOW ARE CIVIL SERVICE EXAMS DEVELOPED?*

Examinations are carefully written by trained technicians who are specialists in the field known as "psychological measurement," in consultation with recognized authorities in the field of work that the test will cover. These experts recommend the subject matter areas or skills to be tested; only those knowledges or skills important to your success on the job are included. The most reliable books and source materials available are used as references. Together, the experts and technicians judge the difficulty level of the questions.

Test technicians know how to phrase questions so that the problem is clearly stated. Their ethics do not permit "trick" or "catch" questions. Questions may have been tried out on sample groups, or subjected to statistical analysis, to determine their usefulness.

Written tests are often used in combination with performance tests, ratings of training and experience, and oral interviews. All of these measures combine to form the best-known means of finding the right person for the right job.

II. HOW TO PASS THE WRITTEN TEST

A. *NATURE OF THE EXAMINATION*

To prepare intelligently for civil service examinations, you should know how they differ from school examinations you have taken. In school you were assigned certain definite pages to read or subjects to cover. The examination questions were quite detailed and usually emphasized memory. Civil service exams, on the other hand, try to discover your present ability to perform the duties of a position, plus your potentiality to learn these duties. In other words, a civil service exam attempts to predict how successful you will be. Questions cover such a broad area that they cannot be as minute and detailed as school exam questions.

In the public service similar kinds of work, or positions, are grouped together in one "class." This process is known as *position-classification*. All the positions in a class are paid according to the salary range for that class. One class title covers all of these positions, and they are all tested by the same examination.

B. *FOUR BASIC STEPS*

1) Study the announcement

How, then, can you know what subjects to study? Our best answer is: "Learn as much as possible about the class of positions for which you've applied." The exam will test the knowledge, skills and abilities needed to do the work.

Your most valuable source of information about the position you want is the official exam announcement. This announcement lists the training and experience qualifications. Check these standards and apply only if you come reasonably close to meeting them.

The brief description of the position in the examination announcement offers some clues to the subjects which will be tested. Think about the job itself. Review the duties in your mind. Can you perform them, or are there some in which you are rusty? Fill in the blank spots in your preparation.

Many jurisdictions preview the written test in the exam announcement by including a section called "Knowledge and Abilities Required," "Scope of the Examination," or some similar heading. Here you will find out specifically what fields will be tested.

2) Review your own background

Once you learn in general what the position is all about, and what you need to know to do the work, ask yourself which subjects you already know fairly well and which need improvement. You may wonder whether to concentrate on improving your strong areas or on building some background in your fields of weakness. When the announcement has specified "some knowledge" or "considerable knowledge," or has used adjectives like "beginning principles of..." or "advanced ... methods," you can get a clue as to the number and difficulty of questions to be asked in any given field. More questions, and hence broader coverage, would be included for those subjects which are more important in the work. Now weigh your strengths and weaknesses against the job requirements and prepare accordingly.

3) Determine the level of the position

Another way to tell how intensively you should prepare is to understand the level of the job for which you are applying. Is it the entering level? In other words, is this the position in which beginners in a field of work are hired? Or is it an intermediate or advanced level? Sometimes this is indicated by such words as "Junior" or "Senior" in the class title. Other jurisdictions use Roman numerals to designate the level – Clerk I, Clerk II, for example. The word "Supervisor" sometimes appears in the title. If the level is not indicated by the title, check the description of duties. Will you be working under very close supervision, or will you have responsibility for independent decisions in this work?

4) Choose appropriate study materials

Now that you know the subjects to be examined and the relative amount of each subject to be covered, you can choose suitable study materials. For beginning level jobs, or even advanced ones, if you have a pronounced weakness in some aspect of your training, read a modern, standard textbook in that field. Be sure it is up to date and has general coverage. Such books are normally available at your library, and the librarian will be glad to help you locate one. For entry-level positions, questions of appropriate difficulty are chosen – neither highly advanced questions, nor those too simple. Such questions require careful thought but not advanced training.

If the position for which you are applying is technical or advanced, you will read more advanced, specialized material. If you are already familiar with the basic principles of your field, elementary textbooks would waste your time. Concentrate on advanced textbooks and technical periodicals. Think through the concepts and review difficult problems in your field.

These are all general sources. You can get more ideas on your own initiative, following these leads. For example, training manuals and publications of the government agency which employs workers in your field can be useful, particularly for technical and professional positions. A letter or visit to the government department involved may result in more specific study suggestions, and certainly will provide you with a more definite idea of the exact nature of the position you are seeking.

III. KINDS OF TESTS

Tests are used for purposes other than measuring knowledge and ability to perform specified duties. For some positions, it is equally important to test ability to make adjustments to new situations or to profit from training. In others, basic mental abilities not dependent on information are essential. Questions which test these things may not appear as pertinent to the duties of the position as those which test for knowledge and information. Yet they are often highly important parts of a fair examination. For very general questions, it is almost impossible to help you direct your study efforts. What we can do is to point out some of the more common of these general abilities needed in public service positions and describe some typical questions.

1) General information

Broad, general information has been found useful for predicting job success in some kinds of work. This is tested in a variety of ways, from vocabulary lists to questions about current events. Basic background in some field of work, such as sociology or economics, may be sampled in a group of questions. Often these are principles which have become familiar to most persons through exposure rather than through formal training. It is difficult to advise you how to study for these questions; being alert to the world around you is our best suggestion.

2) Verbal ability

An example of an ability needed in many positions is verbal or language ability. Verbal ability is, in brief, the ability to use and understand words. Vocabulary and grammar tests are typical measures of this ability. Reading comprehension or paragraph interpretation questions are common in many kinds of civil service tests. You are given a paragraph of written material and asked to find its central meaning.

3) Numerical ability

Number skills can be tested by the familiar arithmetic problem, by checking paired lists of numbers to see which are alike and which are different, or by interpreting charts and graphs. In the latter test, a graph may be printed in the test booklet which you are asked to use as the basis for answering questions.

4) Observation

A popular test for law-enforcement positions is the observation test. A picture is shown to you for several minutes, then taken away. Questions about the picture test your ability to observe both details and larger elements.

5) Following directions

In many positions in the public service, the employee must be able to carry out written instructions dependably and accurately. You may be given a chart with several columns, each column listing a variety of information. The questions require you to carry out directions involving the information given in the chart.

6) Skills and aptitudes

Performance tests effectively measure some manual skills and aptitudes. When the skill is one in which you are trained, such as typing or shorthand, you can practice. These tests are often very much like those given in business school or high school courses. For many of the other skills and aptitudes, however, no short-time preparation can be made. Skills and abilities natural to you or that you have developed throughout your lifetime are being tested.

Many of the general questions just described provide all the data needed to answer the questions and ask you to use your reasoning ability to find the answers. Your best preparation for these tests, as well as for tests of facts and ideas, is to be at your physical and mental best. You, no doubt, have your own methods of getting into an exam-taking mood and keeping "in shape." The next section lists some ideas on this subject.

IV. KINDS OF QUESTIONS

Only rarely is the "essay" question, which you answer in narrative form, used in civil service tests. Civil service tests are usually of the short-answer type. Full instructions for answering these questions will be given to you at the examination. But in case this is your first experience with short-answer questions and separate answer sheets, here is what you need to know:

1) Multiple-choice Questions

Most popular of the short-answer questions is the "multiple choice" or "best answer" question. It can be used, for example, to test for factual knowledge, ability to solve problems or judgment in meeting situations found at work.

A multiple-choice question is normally one of three types—

- It can begin with an incomplete statement followed by several possible endings. You are to find the one ending which *best* completes the statement, although some of the others may not be entirely wrong.
- It can also be a complete statement in the form of a question which is answered by choosing one of the statements listed.
- It can be in the form of a problem – again you select the best answer.

Here is an example of a multiple-choice question with a discussion which should give you some clues as to the method for choosing the right answer:

When an employee has a complaint about his assignment, the action which will *best* help him overcome his difficulty is to
A. discuss his difficulty with his coworkers
B. take the problem to the head of the organization
C. take the problem to the person who gave him the assignment
D. say nothing to anyone about his complaint

In answering this question, you should study each of the choices to find which is best. Consider choice "A" – Certainly an employee may discuss his complaint with fellow employees, but no change or improvement can result, and the complaint remains unresolved. Choice "B" is a poor choice since the head of the organization probably does not know what assignment you have been given, and taking your problem to him is known as "going over the head" of the supervisor. The supervisor, or person who made the assignment, is the person who can clarify it or correct any injustice. Choice "C" is, therefore, correct. To say nothing, as in choice "D," is unwise. Supervisors have and interest in knowing the problems employees are facing, and the employee is seeking a solution to his problem.

2) True/False Questions

The "true/false" or "right/wrong" form of question is sometimes used. Here a complete statement is given. Your job is to decide whether the statement is right or wrong.

SAMPLE: A roaming cell-phone call to a nearby city costs less than a non-roaming call to a distant city.

This statement is wrong, or false, since roaming calls are more expensive.
This is not a complete list of all possible question forms, although most of the others are variations of these common types. You will always get complete directions for

answering questions. Be sure you understand *how* to mark your answers – ask questions until you do.

V. RECORDING YOUR ANSWERS

Computer terminals are used more and more today for many different kinds of exams.

For an examination with very few applicants, you may be told to record your answers in the test booklet itself. Separate answer sheets are much more common. If this separate answer sheet is to be scored by machine – and this is often the case – it is highly important that you mark your answers correctly in order to get credit.

An electronic scoring machine is often used in civil service offices because of the speed with which papers can be scored. Machine-scored answer sheets must be marked with a pencil, which will be given to you. This pencil has a high graphite content which responds to the electronic scoring machine. As a matter of fact, stray dots may register as answers, so do not let your pencil rest on the answer sheet while you are pondering the correct answer. Also, if your pencil lead breaks or is otherwise defective, ask for another.

Since the answer sheet will be dropped in a slot in the scoring machine, be careful not to bend the corners or get the paper crumpled.

The answer sheet normally has five vertical columns of numbers, with 30 numbers to a column. These numbers correspond to the question numbers in your test booklet. After each number, going across the page are four or five pairs of dotted lines. These short dotted lines have small letters or numbers above them. The first two pairs may also have a "T" or "F" above the letters. This indicates that the first two pairs only are to be used if the questions are of the true-false type. If the questions are multiple choice, disregard the "T" and "F" and pay attention only to the small letters or numbers.

Answer your questions in the manner of the sample that follows:

32. The largest city in the United States is
    A. Washington, D.C.
    B. New York City
    C. Chicago
    D. Detroit
    E. San Francisco

1) Choose the answer you think is best. (New York City is the largest, so "B" is correct.)
2) Find the row of dotted lines numbered the same as the question you are answering. (Find row number 32)
3) Find the pair of dotted lines corresponding to the answer. (Find the pair of lines under the mark "B.")
4) Make a solid black mark between the dotted lines.

VI. BEFORE THE TEST

Common sense will help you find procedures to follow to get ready for an examination. Too many of us, however, overlook these sensible measures. Indeed, nervousness and fatigue have been found to be the most serious reasons why applicants fail to do their best on civil service tests. Here is a list of reminders:

- Begin your preparation early – Don't wait until the last minute to go scurrying around for books and materials or to find out what the position is all about.
- Prepare continuously – An hour a night for a week is better than an all-night cram session. This has been definitely established. What is more, a night a week for a month will return better dividends than crowding your study into a shorter period of time.
- Locate the place of the exam – You have been sent a notice telling you when and where to report for the examination. If the location is in a different town or otherwise unfamiliar to you, it would be well to inquire the best route and learn something about the building.
- Relax the night before the test – Allow your mind to rest. Do not study at all that night. Plan some mild recreation or diversion; then go to bed early and get a good night's sleep.
- Get up early enough to make a leisurely trip to the place for the test – This way unforeseen events, traffic snarls, unfamiliar buildings, etc. will not upset you.
- Dress comfortably – A written test is not a fashion show. You will be known by number and not by name, so wear something comfortable.
- Leave excess paraphernalia at home – Shopping bags and odd bundles will get in your way. You need bring only the items mentioned in the official notice you received; usually everything you need is provided. Do not bring reference books to the exam. They will only confuse those last minutes and be taken away from you when in the test room.
- Arrive somewhat ahead of time – If because of transportation schedules you must get there very early, bring a newspaper or magazine to take your mind off yourself while waiting.
- Locate the examination room – When you have found the proper room, you will be directed to the seat or part of the room where you will sit. Sometimes you are given a sheet of instructions to read while you are waiting. Do not fill out any forms until you are told to do so; just read them and be prepared.
- Relax and prepare to listen to the instructions
- If you have any physical problem that may keep you from doing your best, be sure to tell the test administrator. If you are sick or in poor health, you really cannot do your best on the exam. You can come back and take the test some other time.

VII. AT THE TEST

The day of the test is here and you have the test booklet in your hand. The temptation to get going is very strong. Caution! There is more to success than knowing the right answers. You must know how to identify your papers and understand variations in the type of short-answer question used in this particular examination. Follow these suggestions for maximum results from your efforts:

1) Cooperate with the monitor

The test administrator has a duty to create a situation in which you can be as much at ease as possible. He will give instructions, tell you when to begin, check to see that you are marking your answer sheet correctly, and so on. He is not there to guard you, although he will see that your competitors do not take unfair advantage. He wants to help you do your best.

2) Listen to all instructions

Don't jump the gun! Wait until you understand all directions. In most civil service tests you get more time than you need to answer the questions. So don't be in a hurry. Read each word of instructions until you clearly understand the meaning. Study the examples, listen to all announcements and follow directions. Ask questions if you do not understand what to do.

3) Identify your papers

Civil service exams are usually identified by number only. You will be assigned a number; you must not put your name on your test papers. Be sure to copy your number correctly. Since more than one exam may be given, copy your exact examination title.

4) Plan your time

Unless you are told that a test is a "speed" or "rate of work" test, speed itself is usually not important. Time enough to answer all the questions will be provided, but this does not mean that you have all day. An overall time limit has been set. Divide the total time (in minutes) by the number of questions to determine the approximate time you have for each question.

5) Do not linger over difficult questions

If you come across a difficult question, mark it with a paper clip (useful to have along) and come back to it when you have been through the booklet. One caution if you do this – be sure to skip a number on your answer sheet as well. Check often to be sure that you have not lost your place and that you are marking in the row numbered the same as the question you are answering.

6) Read the questions

Be sure you know what the question asks! Many capable people are unsuccessful because they failed to *read* the questions correctly.

7) Answer all questions

Unless you have been instructed that a penalty will be deducted for incorrect answers, it is better to guess than to omit a question.

8) Speed tests

It is often better NOT to guess on speed tests. It has been found that on timed tests people are tempted to spend the last few seconds before time is called in marking answers at random – without even reading them – in the hope of picking up a few extra points. To discourage this practice, the instructions may warn you that your score will be "corrected" for guessing. That is, a penalty will be applied. The incorrect answers will be deducted from the correct ones, or some other penalty formula will be used.

9) Review your answers

If you finish before time is called, go back to the questions you guessed or omitted to give them further thought. Review other answers if you have time.

10) Return your test materials

If you are ready to leave before others have finished or time is called, take ALL your materials to the monitor and leave quietly. Never take any test material with you. The monitor can discover whose papers are not complete, and taking a test booklet may be grounds for disqualification.

VIII. EXAMINATION TECHNIQUES

1) Read the general instructions carefully. These are usually printed on the first page of the exam booklet. As a rule, these instructions refer to the timing of the examination; the fact that you should not start work until the signal and must stop work at a signal, etc. If there are any *special* instructions, such as a choice of questions to be answered, make sure that you note this instruction carefully.

2) When you are ready to start work on the examination, that is as soon as the signal has been given, read the instructions to each question booklet, underline any key words or phrases, such as *least*, *best*, *outline*, *describe* and the like. In this way you will tend to answer as requested rather than discover on reviewing your paper that you *listed without describing*, that you selected the *worst* choice rather than the *best* choice, etc.

3) If the examination is of the objective or multiple-choice type – that is, each question will also give a series of possible answers: A, B, C or D, and you are called upon to select the best answer and write the letter next to that answer on your answer paper – it is advisable to start answering each question in turn. There may be anywhere from 50 to 100 such questions in the three or four hours allotted and you can see how much time would be taken if you read through all the questions before beginning to answer any. Furthermore, if you come across a question or group of questions which you know would be difficult to answer, it would undoubtedly affect your handling of all the other questions.

4) If the examination is of the essay type and contains but a few questions, it is a moot point as to whether you should read all the questions before starting to answer any one. Of course, if you are given a choice – say five out of seven and the like – then it is essential to read all the questions so you can eliminate the two that are most difficult. If, however, you are asked to answer all the questions, there may be danger in trying to answer the easiest one first because you may find that you will spend too much time on it. The best technique is to answer the first question, then proceed to the second, etc.

5) Time your answers. Before the exam begins, write down the time it started, then add the time allowed for the examination and write down the time it must be completed, then divide the time available somewhat as follows:

- If 3-1/2 hours are allowed, that would be 210 minutes. If you have 80 objective-type questions, that would be an average of 2-1/2 minutes per question. Allow yourself no more than 2 minutes per question, or a total of 160 minutes, which will permit about 50 minutes to review.
- If for the time allotment of 210 minutes there are 7 essay questions to answer, that would average about 30 minutes a question. Give yourself only 25 minutes per question so that you have about 35 minutes to review.

6) The most important instruction is to *read each question* and make sure you know what is wanted. The second most important instruction is to *time yourself properly* so that you answer every question. The third most important instruction is to *answer every question*. Guess if you have to but include something for each question. Remember that you will receive no credit for a blank and will probably receive some credit if you write something in answer to an essay question. If you guess a letter – say "B" for a multiple-choice question – you may have guessed right. If you leave a blank as an answer to a multiple-choice question, the examiners may respect your feelings but it will not add a point to your score. Some exams may penalize you for wrong answers, so in such cases *only*, you may not want to guess unless you have some basis for your answer.

7) Suggestions
   a. Objective-type questions
      1. Examine the question booklet for proper sequence of pages and questions
      2. Read all instructions carefully
      3. Skip any question which seems too difficult; return to it after all other questions have been answered
      4. Apportion your time properly; do not spend too much time on any single question or group of questions
      5. Note and underline key words – *all, most, fewest, least, best, worst, same, opposite*, etc.
      6. Pay particular attention to negatives
      7. Note unusual option, e.g., unduly long, short, complex, different or similar in content to the body of the question
      8. Observe the use of "hedging" words – *probably, may, most likely*, etc.
      9. Make sure that your answer is put next to the same number as the question
      10. Do not second-guess unless you have good reason to believe the second answer is definitely more correct
      11. Cross out original answer if you decide another answer is more accurate; do not erase until you are ready to hand your paper in
      12. Answer all questions; guess unless instructed otherwise
      13. Leave time for review

   b. Essay questions
      1. Read each question carefully
      2. Determine exactly what is wanted. Underline key words or phrases.
      3. Decide on outline or paragraph answer

4. Include many different points and elements unless asked to develop any one or two points or elements
5. Show impartiality by giving pros and cons unless directed to select one side only
6. Make and write down any assumptions you find necessary to answer the questions
7. Watch your English, grammar, punctuation and choice of words
8. Time your answers; don't crowd material

8) Answering the essay question

Most essay questions can be answered by framing the specific response around several key words or ideas. Here are a few such key words or ideas:

M's: manpower, materials, methods, money, management
P's: purpose, program, policy, plan, procedure, practice, problems, pitfalls, personnel, public relations
   a. Six basic steps in handling problems:
     1. Preliminary plan and background development
     2. Collect information, data and facts
     3. Analyze and interpret information, data and facts
     4. Analyze and develop solutions as well as make recommendations
     5. Prepare report and sell recommendations
     6. Install recommendations and follow up effectiveness

   b. Pitfalls to avoid
     1. *Taking things for granted* – A statement of the situation does not necessarily imply that each of the elements is necessarily true; for example, a complaint may be invalid and biased so that all that can be taken for granted is that a complaint has been registered
     2. *Considering only one side of a situation* – Wherever possible, indicate several alternatives and then point out the reasons you selected the best one
     3. *Failing to indicate follow up* – Whenever your answer indicates action on your part, make certain that you will take proper follow-up action to see how successful your recommendations, procedures or actions turn out to be
     4. *Taking too long in answering any single question* – Remember to time your answers properly

IX. AFTER THE TEST

Scoring procedures differ in detail among civil service jurisdictions although the general principles are the same. Whether the papers are hand-scored or graded by machine we have described, they are nearly always graded by number. That is, the person who marks the paper knows only the number – never the name – of the applicant. Not until all the papers have been graded will they be matched with names. If other tests, such as training and experience or oral interview ratings have been given, scores will be combined. Different parts of the examination usually have different weights. For example, the written test might count 60 percent of the final grade, and a rating of training and experience 40 percent. In many jurisdictions, veterans will have a certain number of points added to their grades.

After the final grade has been determined, the names are placed in grade order and an eligible list is established. There are various methods for resolving ties between those who get the same final grade – probably the most common is to place first the name of the person whose application was received first. Job offers are made from the eligible list in the order the names appear on it. You will be notified of your grade and your rank as soon as all these computations have been made. This will be done as rapidly as possible.

People who are found to meet the requirements in the announcement are called "eligibles." Their names are put on a list of eligible candidates. An eligible's chances of getting a job depend on how high he stands on this list and how fast agencies are filling jobs from the list.

When a job is to be filled from a list of eligibles, the agency asks for the names of people on the list of eligibles for that job. When the civil service commission receives this request, it sends to the agency the names of the three people highest on this list. Or, if the job to be filled has specialized requirements, the office sends the agency the names of the top three persons who meet these requirements from the general list.

The appointing officer makes a choice from among the three people whose names were sent to him. If the selected person accepts the appointment, the names of the others are put back on the list to be considered for future openings.

That is the rule in hiring from all kinds of eligible lists, whether they are for typist, carpenter, chemist, or something else. For every vacancy, the appointing officer has his choice of any one of the top three eligibles on the list. This explains why the person whose name is on top of the list sometimes does not get an appointment when some of the persons lower on the list do. If the appointing officer chooses the second or third eligible, the No. 1 eligible does not get a job at once, but stays on the list until he is appointed or the list is terminated.

X. HOW TO PASS THE INTERVIEW TEST

The examination for which you applied requires an oral interview test. You have already taken the written test and you are now being called for the interview test – the final part of the formal examination.

You may think that it is not possible to prepare for an interview test and that there are no procedures to follow during an interview. Our purpose is to point out some things you can do in advance that will help you and some good rules to follow and pitfalls to avoid while you are being interviewed.

What is an interview supposed to test?

The written examination is designed to test the technical knowledge and competence of the candidate; the oral is designed to evaluate intangible qualities, not readily measured otherwise, and to establish a list showing the relative fitness of each candidate – as measured against his competitors – for the position sought. Scoring is not on the basis of "right" and "wrong," but on a sliding scale of values ranging from "not passable" to "outstanding." As a matter of fact, it is possible to achieve a relatively low score without a single "incorrect" answer because of evident weakness in the qualities being measured.

Occasionally, an examination may consist entirely of an oral test – either an individual or a group oral. In such cases, information is sought concerning the technical knowledges and abilities of the candidate, since there has been no written examination for this purpose. More commonly, however, an oral test is used to supplement a written examination.

Who conducts interviews?

The composition of oral boards varies among different jurisdictions. In nearly all, a representative of the personnel department serves as chairman. One of the members of the board may be a representative of the department in which the candidate would work. In some cases, "outside experts" are used, and, frequently, a businessman or some other representative of the general public is asked to serve. Labor and management or other special groups may be represented. The aim is to secure the services of experts in the appropriate field.

However the board is composed, it is a good idea (and not at all improper or unethical) to ascertain in advance of the interview who the members are and what groups they represent. When you are introduced to them, you will have some idea of their backgrounds and interests, and at least you will not stutter and stammer over their names.

What should be done before the interview?

While knowledge about the board members is useful and takes some of the surprise element out of the interview, there is other preparation which is more substantive. It *is* possible to prepare for an oral interview – in several ways:

1) Keep a copy of your application and review it carefully before the interview

This may be the only document before the oral board, and the starting point of the interview. Know what education and experience you have listed there, and the sequence and dates of all of it. Sometimes the board will ask you to review the highlights of your experience for them; you should not have to hem and haw doing it.

2) Study the class specification and the examination announcement

Usually, the oral board has one or both of these to guide them. The qualities, characteristics or knowledges required by the position sought are stated in these documents. They offer valuable clues as to the nature of the oral interview. For example, if the job involves supervisory responsibilities, the announcement will usually indicate that knowledge of modern supervisory methods and the qualifications of the candidate as a supervisor will be tested. If so, you can expect such questions, frequently in the form of a hypothetical situation which you are expected to solve. NEVER go into an oral without knowledge of the duties and responsibilities of the job you seek.

3) Think through each qualification required

Try to visualize the kind of questions you would ask if you were a board member. How well could you answer them? Try especially to appraise your own knowledge and background in each area, *measured against the job sought*, and identify any areas in which you are weak. Be critical and realistic – do not flatter yourself.

4) Do some general reading in areas in which you feel you may be weak

For example, if the job involves supervision and your past experience has NOT, some general reading in supervisory methods and practices, particularly in the field of human relations, might be useful. Do NOT study agency procedures or detailed manuals. The oral board will be testing your understanding and capacity, not your memory.

5) Get a good night's sleep and watch your general health and mental attitude

You will want a clear head at the interview. Take care of a cold or any other minor ailment, and of course, no hangovers.

What should be done on the day of the interview?

Now comes the day of the interview itself. Give yourself plenty of time to get there. Plan to arrive somewhat ahead of the scheduled time, particularly if your appointment is in the fore part of the day. If a previous candidate fails to appear, the board might be ready for you a bit early. By early afternoon an oral board is almost invariably behind schedule if there are many candidates, and you may have to wait. Take along a book or magazine to read, or your application to review, but leave any extraneous material in the waiting room when you go in for your interview. In any event, relax and compose yourself.

The matter of dress is important. The board is forming impressions about you – from your experience, your manners, your attitude, and your appearance. Give your personal appearance careful attention. Dress your best, but not your flashiest. Choose conservative, appropriate clothing, and be sure it is immaculate. This is a business interview, and your appearance should indicate that you regard it as such. Besides, being well groomed and properly dressed will help boost your confidence.

Sooner or later, someone will call your name and escort you into the interview room. *This is it.* From here on you are on your own. It is too late for any more preparation. But remember, you asked for this opportunity to prove your fitness, and you are here because your request was granted.

What happens when you go in?

The usual sequence of events will be as follows: The clerk (who is often the board stenographer) will introduce you to the chairman of the oral board, who will introduce you to the other members of the board. Acknowledge the introductions before you sit down. Do not be surprised if you find a microphone facing you or a stenotypist sitting by. Oral interviews are usually recorded in the event of an appeal or other review.

Usually the chairman of the board will open the interview by reviewing the highlights of your education and work experience from your application – primarily for the benefit of the other members of the board, as well as to get the material into the record. Do not interrupt or comment unless there is an error or significant misinterpretation; if that is the case, do not hesitate. But do not quibble about insignificant matters. Also, he will usually ask you some question about your education, experience or your present job – partly to get you to start talking and to establish the interviewing "rapport." He may start the actual questioning, or turn it over to one of the other members. Frequently, each member undertakes the questioning on a particular area, one in which he is perhaps most competent, so you can expect each member to participate in the examination. Because time is limited, you may also expect some rather abrupt switches in the direction the questioning takes, so do not be upset by it. Normally, a board member will not pursue a single line of questioning unless he discovers a particular strength or weakness.

After each member has participated, the chairman will usually ask whether any member has any further questions, then will ask you if you have anything you wish to add. Unless you are expecting this question, it may floor you. Worse, it may start you off on an extended, extemporaneous speech. The board is not usually seeking more information. The question is principally to offer you a last opportunity to present further qualifications or to indicate that you have nothing to add. So, if you feel that a significant qualification or characteristic has been overlooked, it is proper to point it out in a sentence or so. Do not compliment the board on the thoroughness of their examination – they have been sketchy, and you know it. If you wish, merely say, "No thank you, I have nothing further to add." This is a point where you can "talk yourself out" of a good impression or fail to present an important bit of information. Remember, *you close the interview yourself.*

The chairman will then say, "That is all, Mr. _____, thank you." Do not be startled; the interview is over, and quicker than you think. Thank him, gather your belongings and take your leave. Save your sigh of relief for the other side of the door.

How to put your best foot forward

Throughout this entire process, you may feel that the board individually and collectively is trying to pierce your defenses, seek out your hidden weaknesses and embarrass and confuse you. Actually, this is not true. They are obliged to make an appraisal of your qualifications for the job you are seeking, and they want to see you in your best light. Remember, they must interview all candidates and a non-cooperative candidate may become a failure in spite of their best efforts to bring out his qualifications. Here are 15 suggestions that will help you:

1) Be natural – Keep your attitude confident, not cocky

If you are not confident that you can do the job, do not expect the board to be. Do not apologize for your weaknesses, try to bring out your strong points. The board is interested in a positive, not negative, presentation. Cockiness will antagonize any board member and make him wonder if you are covering up a weakness by a false show of strength.

2) Get comfortable, but don't lounge or sprawl

Sit erectly but not stiffly. A careless posture may lead the board to conclude that you are careless in other things, or at least that you are not impressed by the importance of the occasion. Either conclusion is natural, even if incorrect. Do not fuss with your clothing, a pencil or an ashtray. Your hands may occasionally be useful to emphasize a point; do not let them become a point of distraction.

3) Do not wisecrack or make small talk

This is a serious situation, and your attitude should show that you consider it as such. Further, the time of the board is limited – they do not want to waste it, and neither should you.

4) Do not exaggerate your experience or abilities

In the first place, from information in the application or other interviews and sources, the board may know more about you than you think. Secondly, you probably will not get away with it. An experienced board is rather adept at spotting such a situation, so do not take the chance.

5) If you know a board member, do not make a point of it, yet do not hide it

Certainly you are not fooling him, and probably not the other members of the board. Do not try to take advantage of your acquaintanceship – it will probably do you little good.

6) Do not dominate the interview

Let the board do that. They will give you the clues – do not assume that you have to do all the talking. Realize that the board has a number of questions to ask you, and do not try to take up all the interview time by showing off your extensive knowledge of the answer to the first one.

7) Be attentive

You only have 20 minutes or so, and you should keep your attention at its sharpest throughout. When a member is addressing a problem or question to you, give him your undivided attention. Address your reply principally to him, but do not exclude the other board members.

8) Do not interrupt

A board member may be stating a problem for you to analyze. He will ask you a question when the time comes. Let him state the problem, and wait for the question.

9) Make sure you understand the question

Do not try to answer until you are sure what the question is. If it is not clear, restate it in your own words or ask the board member to clarify it for you. However, do not haggle about minor elements.

10) Reply promptly but not hastily

A common entry on oral board rating sheets is "candidate responded readily," or "candidate hesitated in replies." Respond as promptly and quickly as you can, but do not jump to a hasty, ill-considered answer.

11) Do not be peremptory in your answers

A brief answer is proper – but do not fire your answer back. That is a losing game from your point of view. The board member can probably ask questions much faster than you can answer them.

12) Do not try to create the answer you think the board member wants

He is interested in what kind of mind you have and how it works – not in playing games. Furthermore, he can usually spot this practice and will actually grade you down on it.

13) Do not switch sides in your reply merely to agree with a board member

Frequently, a member will take a contrary position merely to draw you out and to see if you are willing and able to defend your point of view. Do not start a debate, yet do not surrender a good position. If a position is worth taking, it is worth defending.

14) Do not be afraid to admit an error in judgment if you are shown to be wrong

The board knows that you are forced to reply without any opportunity for careful consideration. Your answer may be demonstrably wrong. If so, admit it and get on with the interview.

15) Do not dwell at length on your present job

The opening question may relate to your present assignment. Answer the question but do not go into an extended discussion. You are being examined for a *new* job, not your present one. As a matter of fact, try to phrase ALL your answers in terms of the job for which you are being examined.

Basis of Rating

Probably you will forget most of these "do's" and "don'ts" when you walk into the oral interview room. Even remembering them all will not ensure you a passing grade. Perhaps you did not have the qualifications in the first place. But remembering them will help you to put your best foot forward, without treading on the toes of the board members.

Rumor and popular opinion to the contrary notwithstanding, an oral board wants you to make the best appearance possible. They know you are under pressure – but they also want to see how you respond to it as a guide to what your reaction would be under the pressures of the job you seek. They will be influenced by the degree of poise you display, the personal traits you show and the manner in which you respond.

ABOUT THIS BOOK

This book contains tests divided into Examination Sections. Go through each test, answering every question in the margin. At the end of each test look at the answer key and check your answers. On the ones you got wrong, look at the right answer choice and learn. Do not fill in the answers first. Do not memorize the questions and answers, but understand the answer and principles involved. On your test, the questions will likely be different from the samples. Questions are changed and new ones added. If you understand these past questions you should have success with any changes that arise. Tests may consist of several types of questions. We have additional books on each subject should more study be advisable or necessary for you. Finally, the more you study, the better prepared you will be. This book is intended to be the last thing you study before you walk into the examination room. Prior study of relevant texts is also recommended. NLC publishes some of these in our Fundamental Series. Knowledge and good sense are important factors in passing your exam. Good luck also helps. So now study this Passbook, absorb the material contained within and take that knowledge into the examination. Then do your best to pass that exam.

EXAMINATION SECTION

EXAMINATION SECTION
TEST 1

DIRECTIONS: Each question or incomplete statement is followed by several suggested answers or completions. Select the one that BEST answers the question or completes the statement. *PRINT THE LETTER OF THE CORRECT ANSWER IN THE SPACE AT THE RIGHT.*

1. Soft iron is MOST suitable for use in a   1.____

    A. permanent magnet   B. natural magnet
    C. temporary magnet   D. magneto

2. Static electricity is MOST often produced by   2.____

    A. pressure   B. magnetism   C. heat   D. friction

3. A fundamental law of electricity is that the current in a circuit is   3.____

    A. inversely proportional to the voltage
    B. equal to the voltage
    C. directly proportional to the resistance
    D. directly proportional to the voltage

4. A substance is classed as a magnet if it has   4.____

    A. the ability to conduct lines of force
    B. the property of high permeability
    C. the property of magnetism
    D. a high percentage of iron in its composition

5. If a compass is placed at the center of a bar magnet, the compass needle   5.____

    A. *points* to the geographic south pole
    B. *points* to the geographic north pole
    C. *alines* itself parallel to the bar
    D. *alines* itself perpendicular to the bar

6. When electricity is produced by heat in an iron-and-copper thermocouple, electrons   6.____
move from

    A. north to south
    B. the hot junction, through the copper, across the cold junction to the iron, and then
        to the hot junction
    C. the hot junction, through the iron, across the cold junction to the copper, and then
        return through the copper to the hot junction
    D. east to west

7. The four factors affecting the resistance of a wire are its   7.____

    A. length, material, diameter, and temperature
    B. size, length, material, and insulation
    C. length, size, relative resistance, and material
    D. size, insulation, relative resistance, and material

8. Electricity in a battery is produced by   8.____

    A. chemical action
    B. chemical reaction
    C. a chemical acting upon metallic plates
    D. all of the above

9. Resistance is ALWAYS measured in   9.____

    A. coulombs   B. henrys   C. ohms   D. megohms

10. The magnetic pole that points northward on a compass   10.____

    A. is called the north pole
    B. is actually a south magnetic pole
    C. points to the north magnetic pole of the earth
    D. indicates the direction of the north geographic pole

11. Of the six methods of producing a voltage, which is the LEAST used?   11.____

    A. Chemical action   B. Heat
    C. Friction   D. Pressure

12. As the temperature of carbon is increased, its resistance will   12.____

    A. increase   B. decrease
    C. remain constant   D. double

13. Around a magnet, the external lines of force   13.____

    A. leave the magnet from the north pole and enter the south pole
    B. often cross one another
    C. leave the magnet from the south pole and enter the north pole
    D. may be broken by a piece of iron shielding

14. When a voltage is applied to a conductor, free electrons   14.____

    A. are forced into the nucleus of their atom
    B. are impelled along the conductor
    C. unite with protons
    D. cease their movement

15. When the molecules of a substance are altered, the action is referred to as   15.____

    A. thermal   B. photoelectric
    C. electrical   D. chemical

16. When matter is separated into individual atoms, it   16.____

    A. has undergone a physical change only
    B. has been reduced to its basic chemicals
    C. retains its original characteristics
    D. has been reduced to its basic elements

17. MOST permanent magnets and all electro-magnets are

    A. classed as natural magnets
    B. manufactured in various shapes from lodestone
    C. classed as artificial magnets
    D. manufactured in various shapes from magnetite

17.____

18. When a conductor moves across a magnetic field,

    A. a voltage is induced in the conductor
    B. a current is induced in the conductor
    C. both current and voltage are induced in the conductor
    D. neither a voltage nor a current is induced

18.____

19. The nucleus of an atom contains

    A. electrons and neutrons
    B. protons and neutrons
    C. protons and electrons
    D. protons, electrons, and neutrons

19.____

20. An alnico artificial magnet is composed of

    A. magnetite, steel, and nickel
    B. cobalt, nickel, and varnish
    C. aluminum, copper, and cobalt
    D. aluminum, nickel, and cobalt

20.____

21. A material that acts as an insulator for magnetic flux is

    A. glass   B. aluminum
    C. soft iron   D. unknown today

21.____

22. The force acting through the distance between two dissimilarly-charged bodies

    A. is a chemical force
    B. is referred to as a magnetic field
    C. constitutes a flow of ions
    D. is referred to as an electrostatic field

22.____

23. An atom that has lost or gained electrons

    A. is negatively charged   B. has a positive charge
    C. is said to be ionized   D. becomes electrically neutral

23.____

24. Which of the following is considered to be the BEST conductor?

    A. Zinc   B. Copper   C. Aluminum   D. Silver

24.____

25. As the temperature increases, the resistance of most conductors also increases. A conductor that is an EXCEPTION to this is

    A. aluminum   B. carbon   C. copper   D. brass

25.____

KEY (CORRECT ANSWERS)

1.	C	11.	C
2.	D	12.	B
3.	D	13.	A
4.	C	14.	B
5.	C	15.	D
6.	B	16.	D
7.	A	17.	C
8.	D	18.	A
9.	C	19.	B
10.	A	20.	D

21.	D
22.	D
23.	C
24.	D
25.	B

TEST 2

DIRECTIONS: Each question or incomplete statement is followed by several suggested answers or completions. Select the one that BEST answers the question or completes the statement. *PRINT THE LETTER OF THE CORRECT ANSWER IN THE SPACE AT THE RIGHT.*

1. The dry cell battery is a _____ cell.   1.____

   A. secondary   B. polarized   C. primary   D. voltaic

2. The electrolyte of a lead-acid wet cell is   2.____

   A. sal ammoniac   B. manganese dioxide
   C. sulfuric acid   D. distilled water

3. A battery which can be restored after discharge is a _____ cell.   3.____

   A. primary   B. galvanic   C. dry   D. secondary

4. Lead-acid battery plates are held together by a   4.____

   A. glass wool mat   B. wood separator
   C. grid work   D. hard rubber tube

5. When mixing electrolyte, ALWAYS pour   5.____

   A. water into acid
   B. acid into water
   C. both acid and water into vat simultaneously
   D. first acid, then water into vat

6. When charging a battery, the electrolyte should NEVER exceed a temperature of   6.____

   A. 125° F.   B. 113° F.   C. 80° F.   D. 40° F.

7. The plates of a lead-acid battery are made of   7.____

   A. lead and lead dioxide   B. lead and lead oxide
   C. silver and peroxide   D. lead and lead peroxide

8. A battery is receiving a normal charge. It begins to gas freely.   8.____
   The charging current should

   A. be increased
   B. be decreased
   C. be cut off and the battery allowed to cool
   D. remain the same

9. A hydrometer reading is 1.265 at 92° F.   9.____
   The CORRECTED reading is

   A. 1.229   B. 1.261   C. 1.269   D. 1.301

10. In the nickel-cadmium battery, KOH is   10.____

   A. the positive plate   B. the negative plate
   C. the electrolyte   D. none of the above

11. When sulfuric acid, H_2SO_4, and water, H_2O, are mixed together, they form a   11._____

    A. gas   B. compound
    C. mixture   D. hydrogen solution

12. How many No. 6 dry cells are required to supply power to a load requiring 6 volts if the   12._____
cells are connected in series?

    A. Two   B. Four   C. Five   D. Six

13. The ordinary 6-volt lead-acid storage battery consists of how many cells?   13._____

    A. Two   B. Three   C. Four   D. Six

14. A fully-charged aircraft battery has a specific gravity reading of   14._____

    A. 1.210 to 1.220   B. 1.250 to 1.265
    C. 1.285 to 1.300   D. 1.300 to 1.320

15. What is the ampere-hour rating of a storage battery that can deliver 20 amperes continu-   15._____
ously for 10 hours?
_____ ampere-hour.

    A. 20   B. 40   C. 200   D. 400

16. The normal cell voltage of a fully-charged nickel-cadmium battery is _____ volts.   16._____

    A. 2.0   B. 1.5   C. 1.4   D. 1.0

17. The electrolyte in a mercury cell is   17._____

    A. sulfuric acid
    B. KOH
    C. potassium hydroxide, zincate, and mercury
    D. potassium hydroxide, water, and zincate

18. Concentrated sulfuric acid has a specific gravity of   18._____

    A. 1.285   B. 1.300   C. 1.830   D. 2.400

19. The number of negative plates in a lead-acid cell is ALWAYS _____ of positive plates.   19._____

    A. one greater than the number
    B. equal to the number
    C. one less than the number
    D. double the number

20. A lead-acid battery is considered fully charged when the specific gravity readings of all   20._____
cells taken at half-hour intervals show no change for _____ hour(s).

    A. four   B. three   C. two   D. one

KEY (CORRECT ANSWERS)

1.	C	11.	C
2.	C	12.	B
3.	D	13.	B
4.	C	14.	C
5.	B	15.	C
6.	A	16.	C
7.	D	17.	D
8.	B	18.	C
9.	C	19.	A
10.	C	20.	A

TEST 3

DIRECTIONS: Each question or incomplete statement is followed by several suggested answers or completions. Select the one that BEST answers the question or completes the statement. *PRINT THE LETTER OF THE CORRECT ANSWER IN THE SPACE AT THE RIGHT.*

1. In which direction does current flow in an electrical circuit?   1.____

    A. - to + externally, + to - internally
    B. + to - externally, + to - internally
    C. - to + externally, - to + internally
    D. + to - externally, - to + internally

2. Given the formula $P = E^2/R$, solve for E.   2.____

    A. $E = \sqrt{ER}$ B. $E = \sqrt{PR}$ C. $E = IR$ D. $E = \sqrt{P/R}$

3. Resistance in the power formula equals   3.____

    A. $R = \sqrt{I/P}$ B. $R = E/I$ C. $R = \sqrt{P \times 1}$ D. $R = E^2/P$

4. One joule is equal to   4.____

    A. 1 watt second   B. 10 watt seconds
    C. 1 watt minute   D. 10 watt minutes

5. A lamp has a source voltage of 110 v. and a current of 0.9 amps. What is the resistance of the lamp?   5.____

    A. 12.22 Ω   B. 122.2 Ω   C. 0.008 Ω   D. 0.08 Ω

6. In accordance with Ohm's law, the relationship between current and voltage in a simple circuit is that the   6.____

    A. current varies inversely with the resistance if the voltage is held constant
    B. voltage varies as the square of the applied e.m.f.
    C. current varies directly with the applied voltage if the resistance is held constant
    D. voltage varies inversely as the current if the resistance is held constant

7. The current needed to operate a soldering iron which has a rating of 600 watts at 110 volts is   7.____

    A. 0.182 a.   B. 5.455 a.   C. 18.200 a.   D. 66.000 a.

8. In electrical circuits, the time rate of doing work is expressed in   8.____

    A. volts   B. amperes   C. watts   D. ohms

9. If the resistance is held constant, what is the relationship between power and voltage in a simple circuit?   9.____

    A. Resistance must be varied to show a true relationship.
    B. Power will vary as the square of the applied voltage.
    C. Voltage will vary inversely proportional to power.
    D. Power will vary directly with voltage.

10. How many watts are there in 1 horsepower?   10.____

    A. 500   B. 640   C. 746   D. 1,000

11. What formula is used to find watt-hours?   11.____

    A. $E \times T$ B. $E \times I \times T$ C. $E \times I \times \sqrt{\theta}$ D. $E \times I^2$

12. What is the resistance of the circuit   12.____
    shown at the right?

    A. $4.8\,\Omega$

    B. $12.0\,\Omega$

    C. $48\,\Omega$

    D. $120\,\Omega$

$I_T = 0.2$ AMP.

24V

R = ?

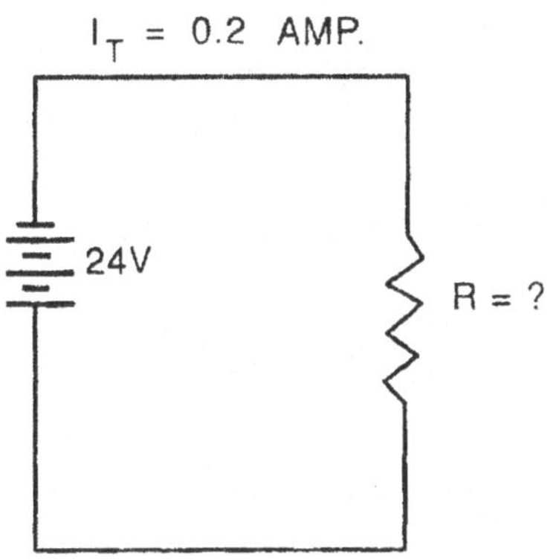

13. In the figure at the right, solve for I_T.   13.____
    A. 0.5 a.
    B. 1 a.
    C. 13 a.
    D. 169 a.

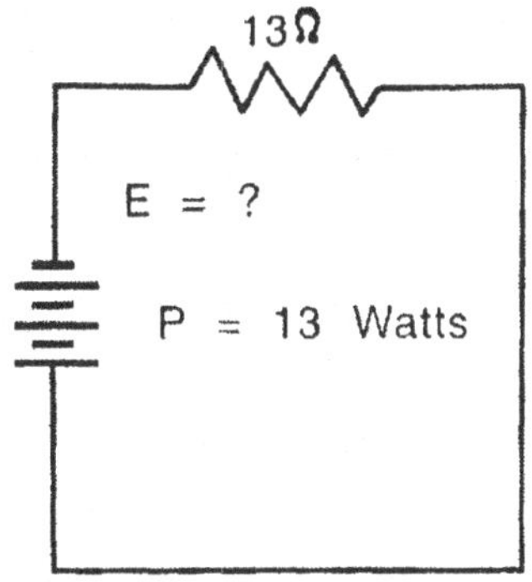

$13\,\Omega$

$E = ?$

$P = 13$ Watts

14. A simple circuit consists of one power source,   14.____

    A. and one power consuming device
    B. one power consuming device, and connecting wiring
    C. protective device, and control device
    D. one power consuming device, and protective device

15. The device used in circuits to prevent damage from overloads is called a   15.____

    A. fuse   B. switch   C. resistor   D. connector

16. What happens in a series circuit when the voltage remains constant and the resistance   16.____
    increases?
    Current

    A. increases   B. decreases
    C. remains the same   D. increases by the square

9

17. Other factors remaining constant, what would be the effect on the current flow in a given circuit if the applied potential were doubled?
It would   17.____

    A. double   B. remain the same
    C. be divided by two   D. be divided by four

18. Which of the following procedures can be used to calculate the resistance of a load?   18.____

    A. *Multiply* the voltage across the load by the square of the current through the load
    B. *Divide* the current through the load by the voltage across the load
    C. *Multiply* the voltage across the load by the current through the load
    D. *Divide* the voltage across the load by the current through the load

19. A cockpit light operates from a 24-volt d-c supply and uses 72 watts of power. The current flowing through the bulb is _____ amps.   19.____

    A. 0.33   B. 3   C. 600   D. 1,728

20. If the resistance is held constant, what happens to power if the current is doubled?
Power is   20.____

    A. doubled   B. multiplied by 4
    C. halved   D. divided by 4

———

KEY (CORRECT ANSWERS)

1.	A		11.	B
2.	B		12.	D
3.	D		13.	B
4.	A		14.	B
5.	B		15.	A
6.	C		16.	B
7.	B		17.	A
8.	C		18.	D
9.	B		19.	B
10.	C		20.	B

———

TEST 4

DIRECTIONS: Each question or incomplete statement is followed by several suggested answers or completions. Select the one that BEST answers the question or completes the statement. *PRINT THE LETTER OF THE CORRECT ANSWER IN THE SPACE AT THE RIGHT.*

1. If a circuit is constructed so as to allow the electrons to follow only one possible path, the circuit is called a(n) _____ circuit.

    A. series-parallel
    C. series
    B. incomplete
    D. parallel

1._____

2. According to Kirchhoff's Law of Voltages, the algebraic sum of all the voltages in a series circuit is equal to

    A. zero
    B. source voltage
    C. total voltage drop
    D. the sum of the IR drop of the circuit

2._____

3. In a series circuit, the total current is

    A. always equal to the source voltage
    B. determined by the load only
    C. the same through all parts of the circuit
    D. equal to zero at the positive side of the source

3._____

4.

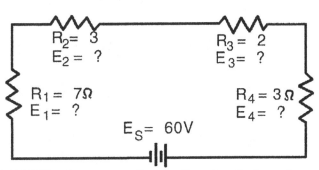

The CORRECT voltage equation for the circuit above is

    A. $E_S + E_1 + E_2 + E_3 + E_4 = 0$
    B. $E_S - E_1 - E_2 - E_3 - E_4 = 0$
    C. $E_S = - E_1 - E_2 - E_3 - E_4$
    D. $-E_S = E_1 + E_2 + E_3 + E_4$

4._____

5. Referring to the circuit shown in Question 4 above, after expressing the voltage drops around the circuit in terms of current and resistance and the given values of source voltage, the equation becomes

    A. $-60 - 71 - 31 - 21 - 31 = 0$
    B. $-60 + 71 + 31 + 21 + 31 = 0$
    C. $60 - 71 - 31 - 21 - 31 = 0$
    D. $60 + 71 + 31 + 21 + 31 = 0$

5._____

6. By the use of the correct equation, it is found that the current (I) in the circuit shown in Question 4 is of positive value. This indicates that the   6.____

    A. assumed direction of current flow is correct
    B. assumed direction of current flow is incorrect
    C. problem is not solvable
    D. battery polarity should be reversed

7.   7.____

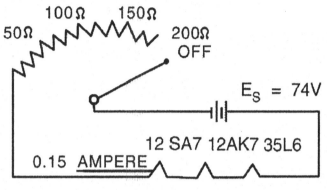

In what position would the variable rheostat in the circuit above be placed in order that the filaments of the tubes operate properly with a current flow of 0.15 ampere? _____ position.

    A. 50 Ω   B. 100 Ω   C. 150 Ω   D. 200 Ω

8. The power absorbed by the variable rheostat in the circuit used in Question 7 above, when placed in its proper operating position, would be _____ watts.   8.____

    A. 112.50   B. 2.25   C. 337.50   D. 450.00

9.   9.____

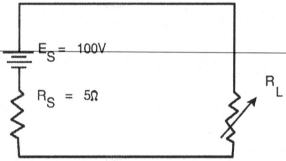

In the circuit above, maximum power would be transferred from the source to the load (R_L) if R_L were set at _____ ohms.

    A. 2   B. 5   C. 12   D. 24

10.

10._____

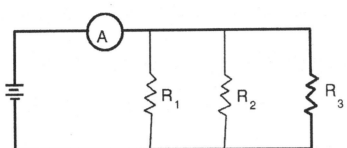

In the circuit above, if an additional resistor were placed in parallel to R₃, the ammeter reading would

A. increase
C. remain the same

B. decrease
D. drop to zero

11. In a parallel circuit containing a 4-ohm, 5-ohm, and 6-ohm resistor, the current flow is

11._____

A. *highest* through the 4-ohm resistor
B. *lowest* through the 4-ohm resistor
C. *highest* through the 6-ohm resistor
D. *equal* through all three resistors

12. Three resistors of 2, 4, and 6 ohms, respectively, are connected in parallel. Which resistor would absorb the GREATEST power?

12._____

A. The 2-ohm resistor
B. The 4-ohm resistor
C. The 6-ohm resistor
D. It will be the same for all resistors

13. If three lamps are connected in parallel with a power source, connecting a fourth lamp in parallel will

13._____

A. *decrease* E_T
C. *increase* E_T

B. *decrease* I_T
D. *increase* I_T

14._____

14.

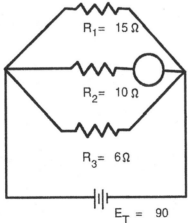

What is the current flow through the ammeter in the circuit shown above?
_____ amps.

A. 4   B. 9   C. 15   D. 28

15.

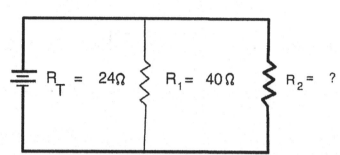

In the circuit shown above, the TOTAL resistance is 24 ohms. What is the value of R_2?
_____ ohms.

   A. 16   B. 40   C. 60   D. 64

15.____

16.

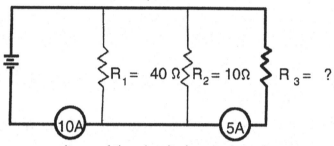

What is the source voltage of the circuit shown above?
_____ volts.

   A. 40   B. 50   C. 100   D. 500

16.____

17. What is the value of R_3 in the circuit shown in Question 16 above?
_____ ohms.

   A. 8   B. 10   C. 20   D. 100

17.____

18.

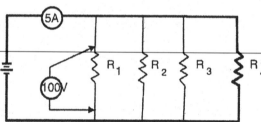

If all 4 resistors in the circuit above are of equal ohmic resistances, what is the value of R_3?
_____ ohms.

   A. 5   B. 20   C. 60   D. 80

18.____

19.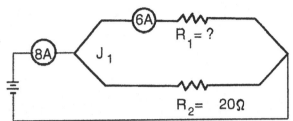

What is the value of the source voltage in the circuit above?
_____ volts

19.____

   A. 20   B. 40   C. 120   D. 160

20.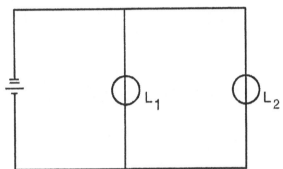

20.____

If Lamp L_2 in the circuit above should suddenly burn out, which of the statements below is CORRECT?

   A. More current would flow through lamp L_1.
   B. Source voltage would decrease.
   C. The filament resistance of lamp L_1 would decrease.
   D. Lamp L_1 would still burn normal.

21. When referring to a circuit's conductance, you visualize the degree to which the circuit

21.____

   A. *permits* or conducts voltage
   B. *opposes* the rate of voltage changes
   C. *permits* or conducts current flow
   D. *opposes* the rate of current flow

22.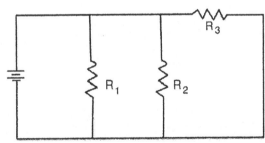

22.____

The TOTAL conductance of the circuit above would be solved by which of the equations?

   A. $G_T - G_1 - G_2 - G_3 = 0$ B. $G_T + G_1 + G_2 + G_3 = 0$
   C. $G_T = G_1 - G_2 - G_3$ D. $G_T = G_1 + G_2 + G_3$

23.

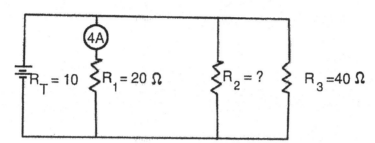

If the resistors in the circuit above are all rated at 250 watts, which resistor or resistors would overheat?

A. R$_1$ B. R$_2$ C. R$_3$ D. All

23._____

24.

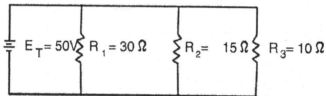

The TOTAL conductance of the circuit above is

A. 0.15G   B. 0.20G   C. 0.50G   D. 0.75G

24._____

KEY (CORRECT ANSWERS)

1.	C		11.	A
2.	A		12.	A
3.	C		13.	D
4.	B		14.	B
5.	C		15.	C
6.	A		16.	A
7.	B		17.	A
8.	B		18.	D
9.	B		19.	B
10.	A		20.	D

21.	C
22.	D
23.	A
24.	B

TEST 5

DIRECTIONS: Each question or incomplete statement is followed by several suggested answers or completions. Select the one that BEST answers the question or completes the statement. *PRINT THE LETTER OF THE CORRECT ANSWER IN THE SPACE AT THE RIGHT.*

1.   The MINIMUM number of resistors in a compound circuit is (are)

   A.   four   B.   three   C.   two   D.   one

1._____

2.

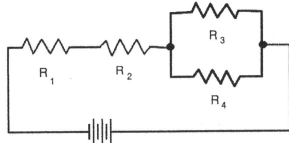

Total resistance of the circuit shown is determined by the formula

2._____

A. $R_1R_2 + \dfrac{R_3R_4}{R_4+R_3}$

B. $R_1+R_2 + \dfrac{R_3+R_4}{R_3R_4}$

C. $R_1+R_2 + \dfrac{R_3R_4}{R_3+R_4}$

D. $R_1+R_2 + (\dfrac{R_3R_4}{R_3+R_4})$

3.

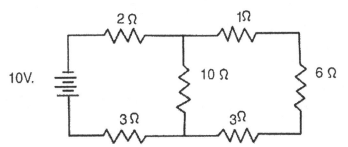

3._____

In the circuit above, what is the value of I_t?

$I_t =$ _____ amp.

   A.   1.14   B.   0.4   C.   0.667   D.   1

4.   In the circuit in Question 3 above, how much power is consumed by the 6-ohm resistor? _____ watts.

4._____

   A.   15   B.   1.5   C.   60   D.   6

5.   A voltage divider is used to

5._____

   A.   provide different voltage values for multiple loads from a single source
   B.   provide several voltage drops in parallel
   C.   increase the voltage to the load at several taps
   D.   provide tap points to alter power supplied

6. The total power supplied to the entire circuit by a voltage divider and 4 loads is the   6._____

   A. sum of the 4 loads
   B. voltage divider minus 4 loads
   C. voltage divider plus the 4 loads
   D. voltage divider only

7. The total voltage of a voltage divider is the   7._____

   A. input voltage minus the load's voltages
   B. the load's voltages only
   C. sum of the input and load voltage
   D. sum of the voltages across the divider

8. An attenuator is   8._____

   A. a network of resistors used to reduce power, voltage, or current
   B. a network of resistors to change the input voltage
   C. also called a pad
   D. used in every power circuit

9. In an attenuator, the resistors are   9._____

   A. adjusted separately
   B. connected in parallel with the load
   C. connected in series with the load
   D. ganged

10. What two conditions may be observed in a bridge circuit?   10._____

   A. T and L network characteristics
   B. No-load and full-load bridge current
   C. Unequal potential and unequal current
   D. Balance and unbalance

11.   11._____

In the circuit above, how much current flows in the resistor and what is its direction?

A. 26 a.; B to A   B. Ia.; A to B
C. 0.273 a.; A to B   D. Ia.; B to A

12. In a three-wire distribution system, an unbalanced situation is indicated by the 12.____

    A. potential of the positive wire being equal to the negative wire
    B. positive wire carrying more amperage than the negative wire
    C. current in the neutral wire
    D. neutral wire carrying the total current

13. 13.____

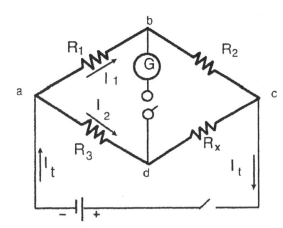

SCHEMATIC
WHEATSTONE-BRIDGE
CIRCUIT

In the figure above, the galvanometer will show zero deflection when

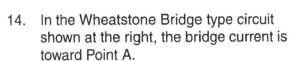

A. $\dfrac{R_1}{R_2} + \dfrac{R_3}{R_x}$
                                B. $R_x = \dfrac{R_1 R_3}{R_2}$

C. $\dfrac{I_1 R_1}{I_2 R_x} = \dfrac{I_2 R_3}{I_1 R_2}$
                     D. $R_x = \dfrac{R_1 R_2}{R_3}$

14. In the Wheatstone Bridge type circuit shown at the right, the bridge current is toward Point A.
The resistance of R_X is

    A. $30\,\Omega$
    B. greater than $45\,\Omega$
    C. $20\,\Omega$
    D. less than $15\,\Omega$

14.____

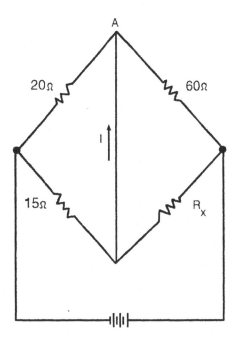

15.

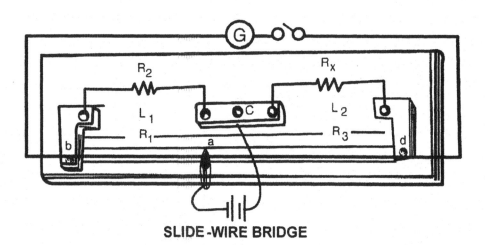

SLIDE-WIRE BRIDGE

In the slide-wire bridge shown above, L_1 is equal to

A. $L_1 = \dfrac{R_2 L_2}{R_1}$

B. $L_1 = \dfrac{R_1 + L_2}{R_2}$

C. $\dfrac{R_2}{R_1 L_2} = L_1$

D. $\dfrac{R_2 L_2}{R_x} = L_1$

15.____

16.

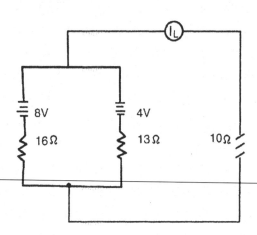

In the circuit above, I line is

A. 4.44 a.   B. 0.444 a.   C. 0.337 a.   D. 5.22 a.

16.____

17. When checking a 3-wire distribution circuit going against the direction of current flow, the IR drop is ALWAYS

A. negative
B. positive
C. not used
D. always in direction of current flow

17.____

18.

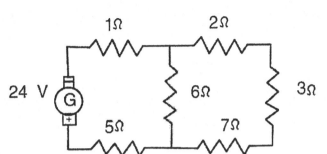

1Ω   2Ω

24 V (G)   6Ω   3Ω

5Ω   7Ω

In the circuit above, the voltage drop across the 3-ohm resistor is _____ volts.

   A. 2.4   B. 24   C. 9.6   D. 0.96

18._____

19.   The resistance of the wire is taken into consideration in the 2- and 3-wire distribution systems because the

   A. source and load are very close
   B. resistance of the wire is the same throughout
   C. load and source are at a considerable distance from each other
   D. load must be decreased in order to determine accurate circuit values

19._____

20.   What is Kirchhoff's second law as applied to 3-wire distribution circuits?

   A. Sum of all the voltages is zero.
   B. Algebraic sum of all the voltages about closed path is zero.
   C. Algebraic sum of all voltage is zero.
   D. All IR drops in the circuit are negative.

20._____

———

KEY (CORRECT ANSWERS)

1.	B	11.	C
2.	C	12.	C
3.	D	13.	A
4.	B	14.	B
5.	A	15.	D
6.	C	16.	C
7.	D	17.	B
8.	A	18.	A
9.	D	19.	C
10.	D	20.	B

———

TEST 6

DIRECTIONS: Each question or incomplete statement is followed by several suggested answers or completions. Select the one that BEST answers the question or completes the statement. *PRINT THE LETTER OF THE CORRECT ANSWER IN THE SPACE AT THE RIGHT.*

1. A mil is what part of an inch?   1._____

    A. 1/10   B. 1/100
    C. 1/1000   D. 1/1,000,000

2. The discharge (electrical leakage) that MIGHT occur from a wire carrying a high potential is called   2._____

    A. arcing   B. sparking
    C. static discharge   D. corona

3. Bare wire ends are spliced by the   3._____

    A. western union method   B. rat-tail joint method
    C. fixture joint method   D. all of the above

4. What is a unit conductor called that has a length of one foot and a cross-sectional area of one circular mil?   4._____

    A. Square mil   B. Circular mil
    C. Circular mil foot   D. Square mil foot

5. The induction-type soldering iron is commonly known as the   5._____

    A. soldering copper   B. pencil iron
    C. soldering gun   D. resistance gun

6. All good quality soldering irons operate at what temperature?   6._____

    A. 400 - 500° F.   B. 500 - 600° F.
    C. 600 - 700° F.   D. 300 - 600° F.

7. A No. 12 wire has a diameter of 80.81 mils.   7._____
   What is the area in circular mils?
   _____ cm.

    A. 6,530   B. 5,630   C. 4,530   D. 3,560

8. Dielectric strength is the   8._____

    A. opposite of potential difference
    B. ability of a conductor to carry large amounts of current
    C. ability of an insulator to withstand a potential difference
    D. strength of a magnetic field

9. To readily transfer the heat from the soldering iron tip, it FIRST should be   9._____

    A. tinned with solder
    B. allowed to form an oxide film
    C. cleaned with carbon tetrachloride
    D. allowed to heat for 25 minutes

10. A No. 12 wire has a diameter of 80.81 mils.
What is the area in square mils?
_____ square mils.

    A. 2,516.8   B. 5,128.6   C. 6,530   D. 8,512.6

10.____

11. Varnished cambric insulation is used to cover conductors carrying voltages above _____ volts.

    A. 1,000   B. 1,500   C. 15,000   D. 5,000

11.____

12. The solder splicer is used to

    A. prevent the waste of rosin core solder
    B. connect together small lengths of solder
    C. connect two conductors together
    D. none of the above

12.____

13. The conductance of a conductor is the ease with which current will flow through it. It is measured in

    A. ohms   B. mhos   C. henrys   D. amperes

13.____

14. Asbestos insulation loses its insulating properties when it becomes

    A. overaged
    B. overheated
    C. used over a long period of time
    D. wet

14.____

15. How are solderless connectors installed on conductors?

    A. Bolted on   B. Chemical compound
    C. Crimped on   D. All of the above

15.____

16. The factor(s) governing the selection of wire size is (are)

    A. (I^2R loss) in the line
    B. (IR drop) in the line
    C. current-carrying ability of the line
    D. all of the above

16.____

17. Enamel insulated conductors are USUALLY called

    A. magnet wire   B. high voltage wire
    C. low voltage wire   D. transmission lines

17.____

18. The advantage of solderless connectors over soldered-type connectors is that they are

    A. mechanically stronger   B. easier to install
    C. free of corrosion   D. all of the above

18.____

19. The basic requirement of any splice is that it be

19._____

    A. soldered
    B. mechanically and electrically as strong as the conductor that is spliced
    C. made with a splicer
    D. taped

20. The type of tape that is used for electrical circuits having a temperature of 175° F. or above is

20._____

    A. glass cloth
    B. plastic
    C. synthetic rubber compound
    D. impregnated cloth

KEY (CORRECT ANSWERS)

1.	C	11.	C
2.	D	12.	C
3.	D	13.	B
4.	C	14.	D
5.	A	15.	C
6.	B	16.	D
7.	A	17.	A
8.	C	18.	B
9.	A	19.	B
10.	B	20.	A

EXAMINATION SECTION
TEST 1

DIRECTIONS: Each question or incomplete statement is followed by several suggested answers or completions. Select the one that BEST answers the question or completes the statement. *PRINT THE LETTER OF THE CORRECT ANSWER IN THE SPACE AT THE RIGHT.*

Questions 1-6.

DIRECTIONS: Questions 1 through 6 are to be answered on the basis of the circuit diagram below. All switches are initially open.

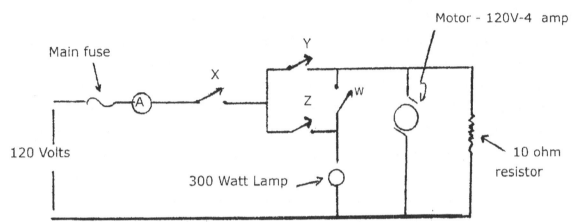

1. To light the 300 watt lamp, the following switches MUST be closed: 1.____

    A. X and Y   B. Y and Z   C. X and Z   D. X and W

2. If all of the switches W, X, Y, and Z are closed, the following will happen: 2.____

    A. The lamp will light and the motor will rotate
    B. The lamp will light and the motor will not rotate
    C. The lamp will not light and the motor will not rotate
    D. A short circuit will occur and the main fuse will blow

3. With 120 volts applied across the 10 ohm resistor, the current drawn by the resistor is   3.____
    _____ amp(s).

    A. 1/12   B. 1.2   C. 12   D. 1200

4. With 120 volts applied to the 10 ohm resistor, the power used by the resistor is _____   4.____
    kw.

    A. 1.44   B. 1.2   C. .144   D. .12

5. The current drawn by the 300 watt lamp when lighted should be APPROXIMATELY   5.____
    _____ amps.

    A. 2.5   B. 3.6   C. 25   D. 36

6. In the circuit shown, the symbol A is used to indicate a (n)   6.____

    A. ammeter   B. *and* circuit
    C. voltmeter   D. wattmeter

7. Of the following materials, the BEST conductor of electricity is   7.____

    A. iron   B. copper   C. aluminum   D. glass

8. The sum of 6'6", 5'9", and 2' 1 1/2" is   8.____

    A. 13'4 1/2"   B. 13'6 1/2"   C. 14'4 1/2"   D. 14'6 1/2"

9.   9.____

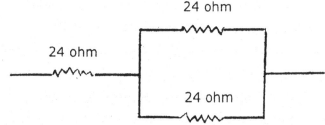

The equivalent resistance of the three resistors shown in the sketch above is _____ ohms.

    A. 8   B. 24   C. 36   D. 72

10.   10.____

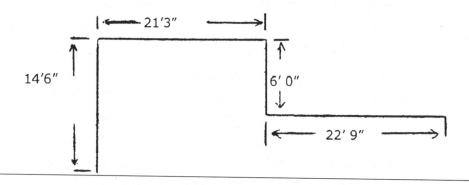

The TOTAL length of electrical conduit that must be run along the path shown on the diagram above is

    A. 63'8"   B. 64'6"   C. 65'6"   D. 66'8"

11. Of the following electrical devices, the one that is NOT normally used in direct current electrical circuits is a (n)   11.____

    A. circuit breaker   B. double-pole switch
    C. transformer   D. inverter

12. The number of 120-volt light bulbs that should NORMALLY be connected in series across a 600-volt electric line is   12.____

    A. 1   B. 2   C. 3   D. 5

13. Of the following motors, the one that does NOT have any brushes is the _____ motor.   13._____

    A. d.c. shunt   B. d.c. series
    C. squirrel cage induction   D. compound

14. Of the following materials, the one that is COMMONLY used as an electric heating ele-   14._____
    ment in an electric heater is

    A. zinc   B. brass
    C. terne plate   D. nichrome

Questions 15-25.

DIRECTIONS: Questions 15 through 25 are to be answered on the basis of the instruments
               listed below. Each instrument is listed with an identifying number in front of it.

         1 - Hygrometer   9 - Vernier caliper
         2 - Ammeter   10 - Wire gage
         3 - Voltmeter   11 - 6-foot folding rule
         4 - Wattmeter   12 - Architect's scale
         5 - Megger   13 - Planimeter
         6 - Oscilloscope   14 - Engineer's scale
         7 - Frequency meter   15 - Ohmmeter
         8 - Micrometer

15. The instrument that should be used to accurately measure the resistance of a 4,700 ohm   15._____
    resistor is Number

    A. 3   B. 4   C. 7   D. 15

16. To measure the current in an electrical circuit, the instrument that should be used is   16._____
    Number

    A. 2   B. 7   C. 8   D. 15

17. To measure the insulation resistance of a rubber-covered electrical cable, the instrument 17._____
    that should be used is Number

    A. 4   B. 5   C. 8   D. 15

18. An AC motor is hooked up to a power distribution box.   18._____
    In order to check the voltage at the motor terminals, the instrument that should be
    used is Number

    A. 2   B. 3   C. 4   D. 7

19. To measure the shaft diameter of a motor accurately to one-thousandth of an inch, the   19._____
    instrument that should be used is Number

    A. 8   B. 10   C. 11   D. 14

20. The instrument that should be used to determine whether 25 Hz. or 60 Hz. is present in   20._____
    an electrical circuit is Number

    A. 4   B. 5   C. 7   D. 8

21. Of the following, the PROPER instrument to use to determine the diameter of the conductor of a piece of electrical hook-up wire is Number

21.____

    A. 10   B. 11   C. 12   D. 14

22. The amount of electrical power being used in a balanced three-phase circuit should be measured with Number

22.____

    A. 2   B. 3   C. 4   D. 5

23. The electrical wave form at a given point in an electronic circuit can be observed with Number

23.____

    A. 2   B. 3   C. 6   D. 7

24. The PROPER instrument to use for measuring the width of a door is Number

24.____

    A. 11   B. 12   C. 13   D. 14

25. A one-inch hole with a tolerance of plus or minus three-thousandths is reamed in a steel block.
The PROPER instrument to use to accurately check the diameter of the hole is Number

25.____

    A. 8   B. 9   C. 11   D. 14

———

KEY (CORRECT ANSWERS)

1.	C	11.	C
2.	A	12.	D
3.	C	13.	C
4.	A	14.	D
5.	A	15.	D
6.	A	16.	A
7.	B	17.	B
8.	C	18.	B
9.	C	19.	A
10.	B	20.	C

21.	A
22.	C
23.	C
24.	A
25.	B

———

TEST 2

DIRECTIONS: Each question or incomplete statement is followed by several suggested answers or completions. Select the one that BEST answers the question or completes the statement. *PRINT THE LETTER OF THE CORRECT ANSWER IN THE SPACE AT THE RIGHT.*

1. The number of conductors required to connect a 3-phase delta connected heater bank to an electric power panel board is   1.____

    A. 2　　　　　B. 3　　　　　C. 4　　　　　D. 5

2. Of the following, the wire size that is MOST commonly used for branch lighting circuits in homes is _____ A.W.G.   2.____

    A. #12　　　　B. #8　　　　C. #6　　　　D. #4

3. When installing electrical circuits, the tool that should be used to pull wire through a conduit is a   3.____

    A. mandrel　　　　　　　　B. snake
    C. rod　　　　　　　　　　D. pulling iron

4. Of the following AC voltages, the LOWEST voltage that a neon test lamp can detect is _____ volts.   4.____

    A. 6　　　　　B. 12　　　　　C. 80　　　　　D. 120

5. Of the following, the BEST procedure to use when storing tools that are subject to rusting is to   5.____

    A. apply a thin coating of soap onto the tools
    B. apply a light coating of oil to the tools
    C. wrap the tools in clean cheesecloth
    D. place the tools in a covered container

6. If a 3 1/2 inch long nail is required to nail wood framing members together, the nail size to use should be   6.____

    A. 2d　　　　　B. 4d　　　　　C. 16d　　　　　D. 60d

7. Of the four motors listed below, the one that can operate only on alternating current is a(n) _____ motor.   7.____

    A. series　　　　　　　　B. shunt
    C. compound　　　　　　　D. induction

8. The sum of 1/3 + 2/5 + 5/6 is   8.____

    A. 1 17/30　　　B. 1 3/5　　　C. 1 15/24　　　D. 1 5/6

9. Of the following instruments, the one that should be used to measure the state of charge of a lead-acid storage battery is a(n)   9.____

    A. ammeter　　　　　　　　B. ohmmeter
    C. hydrometer　　　　　　　D. thermometer

10. If three 1 1/2 volt dry cell batteries are wired in series, the TOTAL voltage provided by the three batteries is _____ volts.   10.____

    A. 1.5   B. 3   C. 4.5   D. 6.0

11. Taking into account time and one-half payment for time over 40 hours of work, the gross pay of an employee who works 43 hours in a week at a rate of pay of $10.68 per hour is   11.____

    A. $427.20   B. $459.24   C. $475.26   D. $491.28

12. The sum of 0.365 + 3.941 + 10.676 + 0.784 is   12.____

    A. 13.766   B. 15.666   C. 15.756   D. 15.766

13. In order to transmit mechanical power between two rotating shafts at right angles to each other, two gears are used. Of the following, the type of gears that should be used are _____ gears.   13.____

    A. herringbone   B. spur
    C. bevel   D. rack and pinion

14. To properly ground the service electrical equipment in a building, a ground connection should be made to _____ the building.   14.____

    A. the waste or soil line leaving
    B. the vent line going to the exterior of
    C. any steel beam in
    D. the cold water line entering

15. The area of the triangle shown at the right is _____ square inches.   15.____
    A. 120
    B. 240
    C. 360
    D. 480

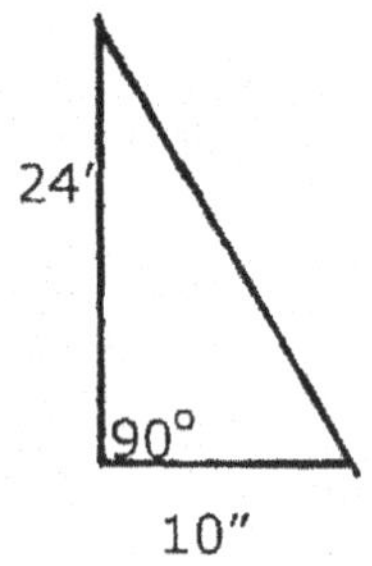

24'   90°   10"

Questions 16-25.

DIRECTIONS: Questions 16 through 25 are to be answered on the basis of the tools shown on the next page. The tools are not shown to scale. Each tool is shown with an identifying number alongside it.

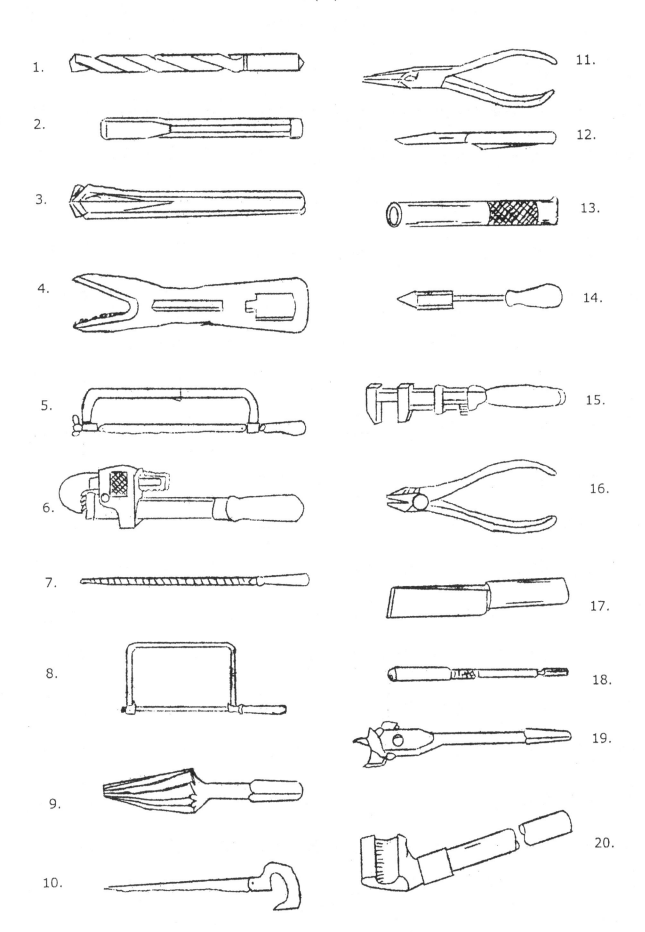

1.

2.

3.

4.

5.

6.

7.

8.

9.

10.

11.

12.

13.

14.

15.

16.

17.

18.

19.

20.

16. The tool that should be used for cutting thin wall steel conduit is Number   16.____

    A. 5   B. 8   C. 10   D. 16

17. The tool that should be used for cutting a 1 7/8 inch diameter hole in a wood joist is Number   17.____

    A. 3   B. 9   C. 14   D. 19

18. The tool that should be used for soldering splices in electrical wire is Number   18.____

    A. 3   B. 7   C. 13   D. 14

19. After cutting off a piece of 3/4 inch diameter electrical conduit, the tool that should be used for removing a burr from the inside of the conduit is Number   19.____

    A. 9   B. 11   C. 12   D. 14

20. The tool that should be used for turning a coupling onto a threaded conduit is Number   20.____

    A. 6   B. 11   C. 15   D. 16

21. The tool that should be used for cutting wood lathing in plaster walls is Number   21.____

    A. 5   B. 7   C. 10   D. 12

22. The tool that should be used for drilling a 3/8 inch diameter hole in a steel beam is Number   22.____

    A. 1   B. 2   C. 3   D. 9

23. Of the following, the BEST tool to use for stripping insulation from electrical hook-up wire is Number   23.____

    A. 11   B. 12   C. 15   D. 20

24. The tool that should be used for bending an electrical wire around a terminal post is Number   24.____

    A. 4   B. 11   C. 15   D. 16

25. The tool that should be used for cutting electrical hookup wire is Number   25.____

    A. 5   B. 12   C. 16   D. 17

_____

KEY (CORRECT ANSWERS)

1.	B		11.	C
2.	A		12.	D
3.	B		13.	C
4.	C		14.	D
5.	B		15.	A
6.	C		16.	A
7.	D		17.	D
8.	A		18.	D
9.	C		19.	A
10.	C		20.	A

21. C
22. A
23. B
24. B
25. C

TEST 3

DIRECTIONS: Each question or incomplete statement is followed by several suggested answers or completions. Select the one that BEST answers the question or completes the statement. *PRINT THE LETTER OF THE CORRECT ANSWER IN THE SPACE AT THE RIGHT.*

1. An electric circuit has current flowing through it. The panel board switch feeding the cir-   1.____
   cuit is opened, causing arcing across the switch contacts.
   Generally, this arcing is caused by

   A. a lack of energy storage in the circuit
   B. electrical energy stored by a capacitor
   C. electrical energy stored by a resistor
   D. magnetic energy induced by an inductance

2. MOST filter capacitors in radios have a capacity rating given in   2.____

   A. microvolts   B. milliamps
   C. millihenries   D. microfarads

3. Of the following, the electrical wire size that is COMMONLY used for telephone circuits is   3.____
   _____ A.W.G.

   A. #6   B. #10   C. #12   D. #22

Questions 4-9.

DIRECTIONS: Questions 4 through 9 are to be answered on the basis of the electrical circuit diagram shown below, where letters are used to identify various circuit components.

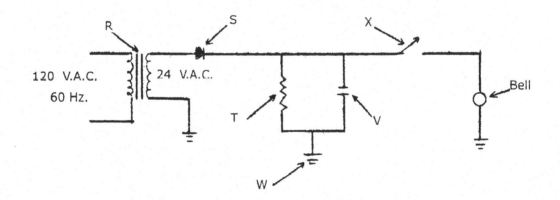

4. The device indicated by the letter R is a   4.____

   A. capacitor   B. converter
   C. resistor   D. transformer

5. The device indicated by the letter S is a   5.____

   A. transistor   B. diode
   C. thermistor   D. directional relay

34

6. The devices indicated by the letters T and V are used together to _____ components of the secondary current.

    A. reduce the AC   B. reduce the DC
    C. transform the AC   D. invert the AC

6._____

7. The letter W points to a standard electrical symbol for a

    A. wire   B. ground
    C. terminal   D. lightning arrestor

7._____

8. Closing switch X will apply the following type of voltage to the bell:

    A. 60 Hz. AC   B. DC
    C. pulsating AC   D. 120 Hz. AC

8._____

9. The circuit shown contains a _____ rectifier.

    A. mercury-arc   B. full-wave
    C. bridge   D. half-wave

9._____

10. A bolt specified as 1/4-28 means the following:
The

    A. bolt is 1/4 inch in diameter and has 28 threads per inch
    B. bolt is 1/4 inch in diameter and is 2.8 inches long
    C. bolt is 1/4 inch long and has 28 threads
    D. threaded portion of the bolt is 1/4 inch long and has 28 threads per inch

10._____

11. When cutting 0.045-inch thickness sheet metal, it is BEST to use a hacksaw blade that has _____ teeth per inch.

    A. 7   B. 12   C. 18   D. 32

11._____

12. To accurately tighten a bolt to 28 foot-pounds, it is BEST to use a(n) _____ wrench.

    A. pipe   B. open end   C. box   D. torque

12._____

13. When bending a 2-inch diameter conduit, the CORRECT tool to use is a

    A. hickey   B. pipe wrench
    C. hydraulic bender   D. stock and die

13._____

14. When soldering two #20 A.W.G. copper wires together to form a splice, the solder that SHOULD be used is _____ solder.

    A. acid-core   B. solid-core
    C. rosin-core   D. liquid

14._____

15. A bathroom heating unit draws 10 amperes at 115 volts.
The hot resistance of the heating unit should be _____ ohms.

    A. .08   B. 8   C. 11.5   D. 1150

15._____

16. Of the following materials, the one that is NOT suitable as an electrical insulator is

    A. glass   B. mica   C. rubber   D. platinum

16._____

17. An air conditioning unit is rated at 1000 watts. The unit is run for 10 hours per day, five days per week.
If the cost for electrical energy is 5 cents per kilowatt-hour, the weekly cost for electricity should be

    A. 25¢   B. 50¢   C. $2.50   D. $25.00

17.____

18. If a fuse is protecting the circuit of a 15 ohm electric heater and it is designed to blow out at a current exceeding 10 amperes, the MAXIMUM voltage from among the following that should be applied across the terminals of the heater is _____ volts.

    A. 110   B. 120   C. 160   D. 600

18.____

19. Before opening a pneumatic hose connection, it is important to remove pressure from the hose line PRIMARILY to avoid

    A. losing air
    B. personal injury
    C. damage to the hose connection
    D. a build-up of pressure in the air compressor

19.____

20. If the scale on a shop drawing is 1/4 inch to the foot, then a part which measures 3 3/8 inches long on the drawing has an ACTUAL length of _____ feet _____ inches.

    A. 12; 6   B. 13; 6   C. 13; 9   D. 14; 9

20.____

21. The function that is USUALLY performed by a motor controller is to

    A. start and stop a motor
    B. protect a motor from a short circuit
    C. prevent bearing failure of a motor
    D. control the brush wear in a motor

21.____

22. Of the following galvanized sheet metal electrical outlet boxes, the one that is NOT a commonly used size is the _____ box.

    A. 4" square   B. 4" octagonal
    C. 4" x 2 1/8"   D. 4" x 1"

22.____

23. When soldering a transistor into a circuit, it is MOST important to protect the transistor from

    A. the application of an excess of rosin flux
    B. excessive heat
    C. the application of an excess of solder
    D. too much pressure

23.____

24. When installing BX type cable, it is important to protect the wires in the cable from the cut ends of the armored sheath.
The APPROVED method of providing this protection is to

    A. use a fiber or plastic insulating bushing
    B. file the cut ends of the sheath smooth
    C. use a connector where the cable enters a junction box
    D. tie the wires into an Underwriter's knot

24.____

25. While lifting a heavy piece of equipment off the floor, a person should NOT   25.____

    A.   twist his body
    B.   grasp it firmly
    C.   maintain a solid footing on the ground
    D.   bend his knees

26. It is important that metal cabinets and panels that house electrical equipment should be   26.____
grounded PRIMARILY in order to

    A.   prevent short circuits from occurring
    B.   keep all circuits at ground potential
    C.   minimize shock hazards
    D.   reduce the effects of electrolytic corrosion

27. A foreman explains a technical procedure to a new employee. If the employee does not   27.____
understand the instructions he has received, it would be BEST if he were to

    A.   follow the procedure as best he could
    B.   ask the foreman to explain it to him again
    C.   avoid following the procedure
    D.   ask the foreman to give him other work

28. Of the following, the BEST connectors to use when mounting an electrical panel box   28.____
directly onto a concrete wall are

    A.   threaded studs   B.   machine screws
    C.   lag screws   D.   expansion bolts

29. Of the following, the BEST instrument to use to measure the small gap between relay   29.____
contacts is

    A.   a micrometer   B.   a feeler gage
    C.   inside calipers   D.   a plug gage

30. A POSSIBLE result of mounting a 40 ampere fuse in a fuse box for a circuit requiring a   30.____
20 ampere fuse is that the 40 ampere fuse may

    A.   provide twice as much protection to the circuit from overloads
    B.   blow more easily than the smaller fuse due to an overload
    C.   cause serious damage to the circuit from an overload
    D.   reduce power consumption in the circuit

KEY (CORRECT ANSWERS)

1.	D		16.	D
2.	D		17.	C
3.	D		18.	B
4.	D		19.	B
5.	B		20.	B
6.	A		21.	A
7.	B		22.	D
8.	B		23.	B
9.	D		24.	A
10.	A		25.	A
11.	D		26.	C
12.	D		27.	B
13.	C		28.	D
14.	C		29.	B
15.	C		30.	C

EXAMINATION SECTION
TEST 1

DIRECTIONS: Each question or incomplete statement is followed by several suggested answers or completions. Select the one that BEST answers the question or completes the statement. *PRINT THE LETTER OF THE CORRECT ANSWER IN THE SPACE AT THE RIGHT.*

1. Which of the following capacitors could be damaged by a reversal in polarity? A(n) _____ capacitor.

    1._____

    A. ceramic   B. paper   C. mica
    D. electrolytic   E. vacuum

2. If the current through a resistor is 6 amperes and the voltage drop across it is 100 volts, what is the approximate value of the resistor in ohm(s)?

    2._____

    A. 1660   B. 166   C. 16.6   D. 1.66   E. 0.0166

3. What is the CORRECT use for an arbor press?

    3._____

    A. Bending sheet metal   B. Driving self-tapping screws
    C. Removing screws   D. Removing "C" rings
    E. Removing bearings from shafts

4. Which one of the following is a tensioning device in bulk-belt-type conveyor systems?
    _____ take-up.

    4._____

    A. Spring   B. Power   C. Hydraulic
    D. Fluid coupled   E. Flexible coupled

5. When $X_L = X_C$ in a series circuit, what condition exists?

    5._____

    A. The circuit impedance is increasing
    B. The circuit is at resonant frequency
    C. The circuit current is minimum
    D. The circuit has no e.m.f. at this time
    E. None of the above

6. Which of the following pieces of information is NOT normally found on a schematic diagram?

    6._____

    A. Functional stage name   B. Supply voltages
    C. Part symbols   D. Part values
    E. Physical location of parts

7. When a single-phase induction motor drawing 24 amps at 120 VAC is re-connected to 240 VAC, what will be the amperage at 240 VAC? _____amps.

    7._____

    A. 6   B. 8   C. 12   D. 24   E. 36

8. Which one of the following meters measures the SMALLEST current?   8.____

    A. Kilometer   B. Milliammeter   C. Microvoltmeter
    D. Millivoltmeter   E. Kilovoltmeter

9. If the current through a 1000-ohm resistor is 3 milliamperes, the voltage drop   9.____
across the resistor is _____ volt(s).

    A. 1   B. 2.5   C. 3   D. 30   E. 300

10. The normally closed contacts of a relay are open when its solenoid is energized
with VDC. The voltage at which the contacts re-close will be

    A. dependent upon the current through the contacts
    B. dependent upon the voltage applied to the contacts
    C. 24 VDC through the coil
    D. more than 24 VDC through the contacts
    E. less than 24 VDC through the coil

11. Electrical energy is converted to mechanical rotation by what component in the
electric motor?

    A. Armature   B. Commutator   C. Field
    D. Start windings   E. Stator

12. Ohm's Law expresses the basic relationship of

    A. current, voltage, and resistance
    B. current, voltage, and power
    C. current, power, and resistance
    D. resistance, impedance, and voltage
    E. resistance, power, and impedance

13. In parallel circuits, the voltage is *always*

    A. variable   B. constant   C. alternating
    D. fluctuating   E. sporadic

14. Which one of the following is used as a voltage divider?

    A. Rotary converter   B. Potentiometer   C. Relay
    D. Circuit breaker   E. Voltmeter

Question 15.

Question 15 is based on the following diagram.

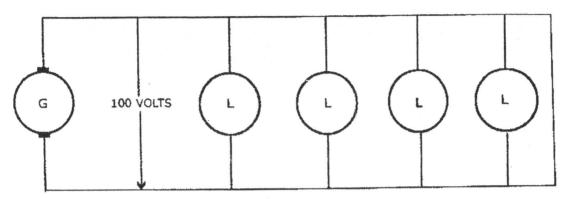

CURRENT IN EACH LAMP 1/2 AMPERE

15. What is the resistance of the entire circuit? _____ ohms.   15.____

   A. 15   B. 25   C. 35   D. 45   E. 50

16. Which one of the following tools is used to bring a bore to a specified   16.____
     tolerance?

   A. Tap   B. Reamer   C. Countersink
   D. Counterbore   E. Center drill

17. The primary function of a take-up pulley in a belt conveyor is to   17.____

   A. carry the belt on the return trip
   B. track the belt
   C. maintain the proper belt tension
   D. change the direction of the belt
   E. regulate the speed of the belt

Question 18.

Question 18 is based on the following diagram.

18. What is the name of the gears?   18.____

   A. Spur external   B. Spur internal   C. Helical
   D. Herringbone   D. Worm

Question 19.

Question 19 is based on the following diagram.

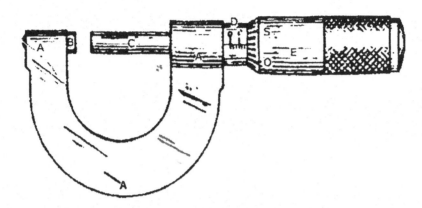

19.   The part labeled D is the   19.____

    A. sleeve   B. thimble   C. frame
    D. anvil   E. pindle

Question 20.

Question 20 is based on the following symbol.

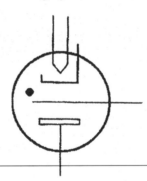

20.   This symbol represents a _____ tube.   20.____

    A. thyratron vacuum   B. thyratron gas
    C. variable-mu vacuum   D. variable-mu gas
    E. vacuum photo

21   A diode can be substituted for which one of the following?   21.____

    A. Transformer   B. Relay   C. Rectifier
    D. Condenser   E. Rheostat

Question 22.

Question 22 is based on the following diagram.

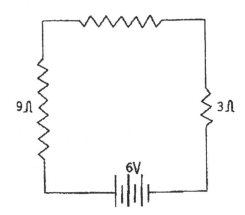

22. The rate of amperes flowing in the circuit is:

    A. .03 1/3   B. .18   C. .24

    D. .30 1/3   E. .33 1/3

22.____

23. The firing point in a thyratron tube is *most usually* controlled by the

    A. cathode   B. grid   C. plate

    D. heater   E. envelope

23.____

Questions 24-25.

Questions 24 and 25 shall be answered in accordance with the diagram below.

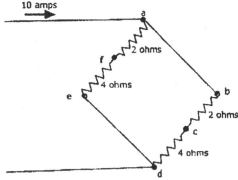

24. With reference to the above diagram, the voltage difference between points c and f is, *most nearly*, in volts,

    A. 40   B. 20   C. 10   D. 5   E. 0

24.____

25. With reference to the above diagram, the current flowing through the resistance c d is, *most nearly*, in amperes,

    A. 10   B. 5   C. 4   D. 2   E. 1

25.____

KEY (CORRECT ANSWERS)

1.	D	6.	E	11.	A	16.	B	21.	C
2.	C	7.	C	12.	A	17.	C	22.	E
3.	E	8.	B	13.	B	18.	A	23.	B
4.	A	9.	C	14.	B	19.	A	24.	E
5.	B	10.	E	15.	E	20.	B	25.	B

EXAMINATION SECTION
TEST 1

DIRECTIONS: Each question or incomplete statement is followed by several suggested answers or completions. Select the one that BEST answers the question or completes the statement. *PRINT THE LETTER OF THE CORRECT ANSWER IN THE SPACE AT THE RIGHT.*

1. Two gears are meshed. The first gear has 20 teeth per inch and is rotating at 500 rpms. What is the speed of the second gear if it has 40 teeth per inch?
   _____ rpms.

      A. 500   B. 400   C. 250   D. 200

   1.____

2. With two meshed gears, the first gear rotates at 100 rpms, the second gear rotates at 2000 rpms and has 10 teeth per inch.
   The first gear has _____ number of teeth per inch.

      A. 200   B. 100   C. 50   D. 150

   2.____

3. Two pulleys are connected. The first pulley has a diameter of 5 inches; the second pulley has a diameter of 15 inches and rotates at 25 rpms.
   The speed of the first pulley is _____ rpms.

      A. 30   B. 75   C. 200   D. 400

   3.____

4. Of two connected pulleys, the first has a radius of 10 inches and rotates at 50 rpms; the second rotates at 25 rpms.
   The diameter of the second pulley is _____ inches.

      A. 40   B. 30   C. 20   D. 10

   4.____

5. Two pulleys are connected. The first pulley rotates at 75 rpms; the second pulley rotates at 100 rpms and has a diameter of 9 inches.
   The diameter of the first pulley is _____ inches.

      A. 10   B. 12   C. 15   D. 20

   5.____

6. Of two connected pulleys, the first pulley has a radius of 12 inches and rotates at 60 rpms; the second pulley has a diameter of 16 inches.
   The speed of the second pulley is _____ rpms.

      A. 1000   B. 1020   C. 1040   D. 1080

   6.____

7. If 16_{10} were converted to base 2, 8, and 16, the results would be _____ base 2, _____ base 8, and _____ base 16, respectively.

      A. 10000; 20; 10   B. 1000; 2000; 20
      C. 20000; 200; 20   D. 2000; 100; 10

   7.____

8. Converting CAF_{16} to base 10 and base 8, the results would be _____ base 10 and _____ base 8, respectively.

      A. 2437; 2567   B. 3247; 6257
      C. 4327; 5267   D. 3427; 2657

   8.____

9. Converting 101011001₂ to base 8, 10, and 16, the results would be _____ base 8, _____ base 10, and _____ base 16, respectively.

   A. 135; 45; 59
   C. 315; 245; 135
   B. 567; 435; 259
   D. 531; 345; 159

9.____

10. If 136₈ were converted to base 2, 10, and 16, the results would be _____ base 2, _____ base 10, and _____ base 16, respectively.

    A. 001011110; 94, 5E
    C. 00100000; 90; 15E
    B. 010100110; 92; 10E
    D. 011001110; 96; 20E

10.____

11. It may be correctly stated that 1000 picofarads are equal to _____ microfarads.

    A. .0001   B. .001   C. .01   D. .1

11.____

12. If 5 megohms were converted to kohms, the result would be _____ kohms.

    A. 1000   B. 2000   C. 4000   D. 5000

12.____

13. 1 nanohenry would convert to _____ millihenries.

    A. .001   B. .0001   C. .00001   D. .0000001

13.____

14. If 7 milliamps were converted to microamps, the answer would be _____ microamps.

    A. 7000   B. 700   C. 70   D. 7

14.____

15. If two resistors are in parallel and are 100 ohms each, the total resistance is

    A. 100   B. 150   C. 50   D. 10

15.____

16. In reference to the circuit in Question 15, if the first resistor has 25 volts DC, (VDC) across it, the second resistor also has 25 VDC across it, and there are no other components in the circuit except for the power source, the total circuit voltage is _____ VDC.

    A. 25   B. 50   C. 250   D. 500

16.____

17. In reference to the circuit in Question 15, if the first resistor has 1 amp on it, and the second resistor also has 1 amp on it, the total circuit amperage is _____ amps.

    A. 1   B. 2   C. 3   D. 4

17.____

18. If two resistors are in series and are 100 ohms each, the total resistance is

    A. 50   B. 100   C. 150   D. 200

18.____

19. In reference to the circuit in Question 18, if the first resistor has 25 VDC across it and the second resistor also has 25 VDC across it, the total circuit voltage is

    A. 50   B. 100   C. 200   D. 500

19.____

20. In reference to the circuit in Question 18, if the first resistor has 1 amp across it and the second resistor also has 1 amp on it, the total circuit amperage is

    A. 1   B. 5   C. 10   D. 15

20.____

21. Where two resistors are in parallel, one is 100 ohms and the other is 300 ohms. The total resistance is _____ ohms.

    A. 25   B. 35   C. 55   D. 75

21._____

22. Three resistors in series are 25 ohms, 50 ohms, and 75 ohms, respectively. The total resistance is _____ ohms.

    A. 25   B. 50   C. 100   D. 150

22._____

23. Two inductors are in parallel; the first is 50 henries and the second is also 50 henries. The total inductance is _____ henries.

    A. 25   B. 50   C. 55   D. 60

23._____

24. Two inductors are in series and the first is 50 henries; the second is 50 henries. The total inductance is _____ henries.

    A. 25   B. 50   C. 75   D. 100

24._____

25. Where two inductors are in parallel, the first is 100 henries and the second is 200 henries. The total inductance is _____ henries.

    A. 50   B. 75   C. 65   D. 100

25._____

_____

KEY (CORRECT ANSWERS)

1. C	6. D	11. B	16. A	21. D
2. A	7. A	12. D	17. B	22. D
3. B	8. B	13. D	18. D	23. A
4. A	9. D	14. A	19. A	24. D
5. B	10. A	15. C	20. A	25. B

_____

TEST 2

DIRECTIONS: Each question or incomplete statement is followed by several suggested answers or completions. Select the one that BEST answers the question or completes the statement. *PRINT THE LETTER OF THE CORRECT ANSWER IN THE SPACE AT THE RIGHT.*

1. Two inductors are in series; the first inductor is 100 henries and the second is 200 henries.
   The total inductance is _____ henries.

   A. 200   B. 300   C. 400   D. 500

   1.____

2. Two capacitors are in parallel; each capacitor is 30 farads.
   The total capacitance is _____ farads.

   A. 60   B. 80   C. 100   D. 200

   2.____

3. Two capacitors are in series; each capacitor is 30 farads. The total capacitance is _____ farads.

   A. 10   B. 15   C. 20   D. 25

   3.____

4. Two capacitors are in parallel; the first is 50 farads and the second is 100 farads.
   The total capacitance is _____ farads.

   A. 50   B. 100   C. 125   D. 150

   4.____

5. Two capacitors are in series; the first is 50 farads and the second is 100 farads.
   The total capacitance is _____ farads.

   A. 33.333   B. 49.999   C. 13.333   D. 25.555

   5.____

6. A resistor's color codes are orange, blue, yellow, and gold, in that order.
   The value of the resistor is _____ kohms ± _____ %.

   A. 200; 2   B. 300; 4   C. 360; 5   D. 400; 7

   6.____

7. If a resistors color codes are red, black, and blue, the value of this resistor is _____ megohms ± _____ %.

   A. 20; 20   B. 40; 80   C. 30; 30   D. 50; 50

   7.____

8. If a resistor's color codes are gray, green, black, and silver, the resistor's value is _____ ohms ± _____ %.

   A. 55; 5   B. 75; 15   C. 85; 10   D. 100; 25

   8.____

9. One complete cycle of a sinewave takes 1000 microseconds. Its frequency is _____ hertz.

   A. 500   B. 1000   C. 2000   D. 5000

   9.____

10. If one complete cycle of a squarewave takes 5 microseconds, its frequency is _____ khertz.

    A. 200   B. 500   C. 700   D. 1000

    10.____

11. What is the PRT (pulse repetition time) of a 50 hertz (hz) sinewave?   11.____
    _____ milliseconds.

     A.   10   B.   20   C.   40   D.   60

12. The PRT of a 20 khz sawtooth signal is _____ megahertz.   12.____

     A.   50   B.   100   C.   200   D.   500

13. If a resistor measures 10 volts and 2 amps across it, the resistance is _____ ohms.   13.____

     A.   0   B.   2   C.   5   D.   10

14. If a 30 ohm resistor measures 10 volts, the power consumed by the resistor is _____   14.____
    watts.

     A.   3000   B.   5000   C.   6500   D.   7000

15. If a 50 ohm resistor measures 4 amps across, the power consumed by it is _____ watts.   15.____

     A.   200   B.   400   C.   600   D.   800

16. If a 100 ohm resistor measures 25 volts across, the current on it is _____ amps.   16.____

     A.   .15   B.   .25   C.   .55   D.   .65

Questions 17-23.

DIRECTIONS: Questions 17 through 23 are to be answered on the basis of the following dia-
               gram.

SERIES CIRCUIT   PARALLEL CIRCUIT

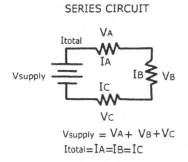 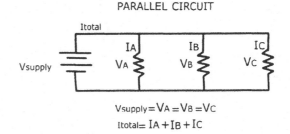

17. In the series circuit above, if Vsupply = 100 VDC, resistor A is 10 ohms, resistor B is 50   17.____
    ohms, and resistor C is 5 ohms, the total circuit current is
    _____ amps.

     A.   1.538   B.   1.267   C.   1.358   D.   1.823

18. In the series circuit shown above, the current across each individual resistor is _____   18.____
    amps.

     A.   .5   B.   1.5   C.   2.5   D.   3.5

19. In the series circuit shown above, the total power drawn by the circuit is _____ watts.   19.____

   A. 140.25   B. 150.75   C. 153.38   D. 173.38

20. In the series circuit shown above, the power drawn from each individual resistor is   20.____
   _____ , _____ , and _____ watts, respectively.

   A. 23.65; 118.27; 11.827   B. 17.567; 123.27; 11.27
   C. 18.627; 145.27; 12.27   D. 21.735; 116.87; 11.83

21. In the parallel circuit shown above, if Vsupply = 100 VDC, resistor A is 10 ohms, resistor   21.____
   B is 50 ohms, and resistor C is 5 ohms, the total circuit current is _____ amps.

   A. 21   B. 27   C. 32   D. 45

22. In the parallel circuit shown above, the total power drawn by the circuit is _____ watts.   22.____

   A. 1200   B. 2300   C. 2700   D. 3200

23. In the parallel circuit above, the power drawn by each individual resistor is _____ watts,   23.____
   respectively.

   A. 100; 200; 2000   B. 200; 400; 5000
   C. 300; 500; 750   D. 450; 600; 1500

24. On an 0-scope display, one cycle of a signal takes up 4 1/2 divisions and the peak-to-   24.____
   peak amplitude of the signal takes up 3 3/4 divisions.
   With the volts/division knob set on 5 volts and the time/division knob set to 5 microseconds, the peak-to-peak amplitude and the frequency of the signal are _____ volts and
   _____ khz, respectively.

   A. 15.75; 100   B. 22.5; 200
   C. 37.5; 350   D. 45.75; 570

25. If a signal that has a peak-to-peak amplitude of 15 volts and a frequency of 5 megaherz   25.____
   is to be observed on an 0-scope with one complete cycle shown, the time/division knob
   and volts/division knob should be set on _____ microseconds and _____ volts per
   division, respectively.

   A. .02; 2   B. .05; 4   C. .07; 3.5   D. 10; 7.5

KEY (CORRECT ANSWERS)

1.	B	6.	C	11.	B	16.	B	21.	C
2.	A	7.	A	12.	A	17.	A	22.	D
3.	B	8.	C	13.	C	18.	B	23.	A
4.	D	9.	B	14.	A	19.	C	24.	B
5.	A	10.	A	15.	D	20.	A	25.	A

EXAMINATION SECTION
TEST 1

DIRECTIONS: Each question or incomplete statement is followed by several suggested answers or completions. Select the one that BEST answers the question or completes the statement. *PRINT THE LETTER OF THE CORRECT ANSWER IN THE SPACE AT THE RIGHT.*

1. If a 3 15/16" shaft wears six thousandths of an inch on the diameter, the new diameter measures MOST NEARLY

    A. 3.932"   B. 3.920"   C. 3.878"   D. 3.861"

1.＿＿＿

2. A drill gage is used for measuring a drill

    A. diameter   B. length
    C. angle of twist   D. cutting angle

2.＿＿＿

3. The reading shown on the micrometer is
    A. 0.174
    B. 0.179
    C. 0.184
    D. 0.189

3.＿＿＿

4. A bulletin on a turnstile specifies that a tension spring, whose spring rate is 33 pounds per inch, be adjusted to exert a tensile force of between 80 and 85 pounds.
If the free length of the spring is 8 1/2", then its FINAL adjusted length when installed should be, in inches, MOST NEARLY

    A. 8 1/4   B. 10 3/8   C. 10 3/4   D. 11

4.＿＿＿

5. The spiral flutes on a drill are provided PRIMARILY to

    A. remove the chips
    B. improve the accuracy of drilling
    C. decrease the weight of the drill
    D. prevent binding on one side of the lip

5.＿＿＿

6. Hex nuts for 5/16" diameter bolts are MOST easily removed from a turnstile mechanism with a ＿＿＿＿＿ wrench.

    A. spanner   B. box   C. strap   D. Stillson

6.＿＿＿

7. If a 10-24 x 3/4 machine screw is not available, the screw which could be MOST easily modified to use in an emergency is a

    A. 12-24 x 1 1/2   B. 12-24 x 3/4
    C. 10-24 x 1   D. 10-24 x 1/2

7.＿＿＿

8. Of the following, the hacksaw blade BEST suited for cutting thin-walled tubing having a thickness of .040" is one which has ＿＿＿＿＿ teeth per inch.

    A. 10   B. 12   C. 18   D. 32

8.＿＿＿

9. Headless set screws are GENERALLY installed by means of a(n)   9.____

    A. torque wrench
    B. box wrench
    C. alien wrench
    D. phillips head screwdriver

10. A pinion has 22 teeth and rotates at 900 rpm. It meshes with a 110-tooth gear.   10.____
    The gear will rotate at _____ rpm.

    A. 4500   B. 900   C. 180   D. 22

Questions 11-14.

DIRECTIONS: Questions 11 through 14 are based on the sketch of a relay circuit shown below. Consult this sketch when answering these questions.

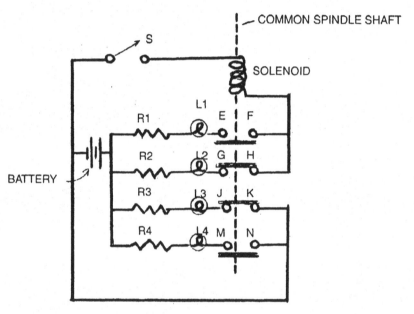

RELAY CIRCUIT

11. With the switch S open, _____ is(are) lit.   11.____

    A. all lights   B. lights L_2 and L_3
    C. light L_3 D. none of the lights

12. When the switch S is closed, _____ are lit.   12.____

    A. all lights   B. lights L_1 and L_4
    C. lights L_2 and L_3 D. none of the lights

13. A PRIME purpose of resistor R_1 is to   13.____

    A. reduce the *hold-in* current in the solenoid
    B. maintain an equalized current flow through the solenoid
    C. prevent arcing across contacts E and F
    D. equalize the current flow through lamp L_2, L_3, and L_4

14. If the solenoid spindle moves back and forth rapidly when the switch S is closed, then the   14._____
    cause of this fault may be that

    A.   the resistor R_2 is open circuited
    B.   the light L_1 is burned out
    C.   the value of resistance R_1 is too low
    D.   both lights L_1 and L_2 are burned out

Questions 15-25.

DIRECTIONS: Questions 15 through 25 are based on the following three view of the Bracket.
                     Consult this drawing when answering these questions.

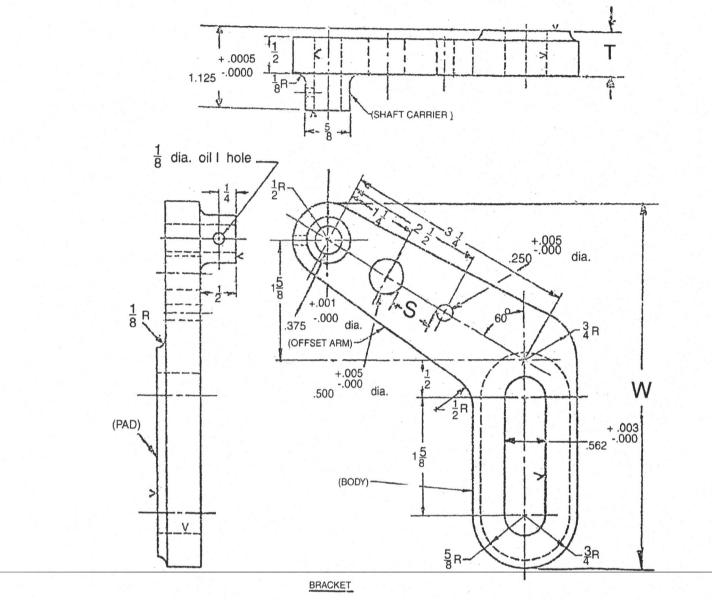

BRACKET

Material - Cast Steel
Machine finish where indicated
Rockwell I C-40
All diamension in inches

15. The hole which PROBABLY will be reamed has a diameter, in inches, of

  +.005   +.001   +.003
  -.000   -.000   -.000

    A. 1/8   B. .250   C. .375   D. .562

16. The slot in the body of the bracket has a width, in inches, of MOST NEARLY

    A. .375   B. 1/2   C. 9/16   D. 3/4

17. The length of the slot *end to end* has a dimension, in inches, of

    A. 1/2   B. 1 5/8   C. 2 3/16   D. 2 3/4

15.____

16.____

17.____

18. The dimension *T,* in inches, is MOST NEARLY   18.____

    A. 1/2   B. 5/8   C. 3/4   D. 7/8

19. Dimension *W,* in inches, is MOST NEARLY   19.____

    A. 4 3/8   B. 5   C. 5 1/8   D. 5 3/8

20. If the shaft that fits in the *shaft carrier* hole has a -001 diameter of .373, the MAXIMUM   20.____
clearance, in inches, between shaft and hole is

    A. .003   B. .004   C. .005   D. .006

21. The expression *Rockwell C-40* indicates the   21.____

    A. type of steel used
    B. hardness of steel used
    C. tensile strength of the material is 40,000 psi
    D. density of the material is 4,000 lbs./cu.ft.

22. If a .561" square block slides in the slot, its maximum permissible stroke, in inches, is   22.____
MOST NEARLY

    A. 9/16   B. 3/4   C. 1 1/16   D. 1 5/8

23. The distance *S,* in inches, between the .500 diameter and .250 diameter holes is MOST   23.____
NEARLY

    A. .750   B. .875   C. .975   D. 1.250

24. If you were making a *GO-NO GO* gage for the .375 diameter hole, the limits of the gage,   24.____
in inches, should be GO - _____ NO GO _____ .

    A. .3745; .3765   B. .3765; .3745
    C. .3753; .3757   D. .3757; .3753

25. If you were checking the accuracy of .562 slot width, the PROPER tool to use is a(n)   25.____

    A. profilometer   B. machinist's scale
    C. depth gage   D. inside vernier caliper

26. To release a tapered shank drill from the drilling machine spindle, it is BEST to use a drill   26.____

    A. center punch   B. drift
    C. file   D. bit

27. The MOST desirable chuck to use for centering an irregularly-shaped work piece in a   27.____
lathe is a _____ chuck.

    A. four-jaw independent   B. drill
    C. three-jaw universal   D. collet

28. The lever length of a torque wrench is 24 inches. If a force of 50 pounds is applied at the   28.____
handle while torquing a nut, then the applied torque, in foot pounds, is

    A. 50   B. 100   C. 400   D. 1200

29. If a maintainer earns $5.42 per hour, and time and one-half for overtime, his gross salary for a week in which he works 2 hours over his regular 40 hours should be

   A. $216.80   B. $224.93   C. $227.64   D. $233.06

29.____

30. A mechanism which will change a continuous clockwise rotational motion into a reciprocating linear motion is a

   A. rack and pinion   B. cam and follower
   C. pinion and gear   D. worm and worm wheel

30.____

31. A brass shear pin is a safety device used in some machines to prevent excessive damage in the event of overloading.
If the shear pin *shears*, it should be replaced by a(n) _____ pin.

   A. identical shear   B. steel
   C. weaker   D. temporary cotter

31.____

32. If crank X shown in the sketch rotates at 20 revolutions per minute, then the member Z should

   A. A. rotate at 20 revolutions per minute
   B. rotate at 10 revolutions per minute
   C. oscillate at 20 cycles per minute
   D. oscillate at 10 cycles per minute

32.____

"Y"   24

CRANK "X"   12   "Z"

6   30

DRAWN TO SCALE

33. Broaching is a general machine shop method for

   A. improving the lubrication of a journal and bearing
   B. producing a non-circular hole
   C. cutting the threads on the O.D. of a shaft
   D. cutting a Woodruff keyway on a shaft

33.____

34. A bronze bushing is to be installed in a pillow block having an I.D. of 3.000-3.001 inches.
An interference fit of 0.001 to 0.003 inches is desired.
The O.D. of the bushing should be MOST NEARLY _____ inches.

   A. 3.002-3.004   B. 3.002-3.003
   C. 2.998-2.999   D. 2.997-3.000

34.____

35. If the driver X shown in the sketch rotates at 5 revolutions per minute, then the follower Y should
   A. rotate at 5 revolutions per minute
   B. oscillate at 5 revolutions per minute
   C. reverse direction
   D. rotate intermittently

35.____

X   Y

36. The sum of the fractions 5/16, 5/8, and 21/32 is MOST NEARLY

   A. 1.491   B. 1.594   C. 1.630   D. 1.642

36.____

37. The MAIN reason for lubricating moving parts of a mechanism is to

    A. remove rust from the surface
    B. prevent injury to the operator
    C. decrease the friction
    D. protect the paint finish

37._____

38. In order to tap a thread to the bottom of a blind hole in a cast bronze housing, taps are used in the following order: _____ tap, _____ tap, _____ tap.

    A. bottoming; taper; plug
    C. taper; plug; bottoming
    B. plug; taper; bottoming
    D. plug; bottoming; taper

38._____

39. When riveting a thin metal to an angle iron, it is good practice to start riveting at the center of the joint, working out in both directions.
This procedure helps to prevent the sheet metal from

    A. buckling
    C. crimping
    B. tearing
    D. contracting

39._____

40. If the thumbscrews in the sketch are both right-hand threads, then to level the arm, the thumb-screws as viewed from above the bubble, should be adjusted by turning

    A. #2 counterclockwise, #1 clockwise
    B. #2 counterclockwise, #1 counterclockwise
    C. #2 clockwise, #1 clockwise
    D. #2 clockwise, #1 counterclockwise

40._____

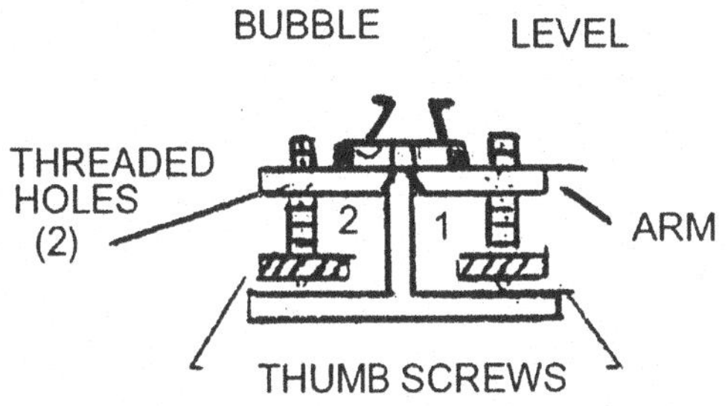

KEY (CORRECT ANSWERS)

1.	A	11.	C	21.	B	31.	A
2.	A	12.	B	22.	C	32.	C
3.	C	13.	A	23.	B	33.	B
4.	C	14.	B	24.	A	34.	B
5.	A	15.	C	25.	D	35.	D
6.	B	16.	C	26.	B	36.	B
7.	C	17.	C	27.	A	37.	C
8.	D	18.	B	28.	B	38.	C
9.	C	19.	B	29.	D	39.	A
10.	C	20.	B	30.	B	40.	A

TEST 2

DIRECTIONS: Each question or incomplete statement is followed by several suggested answers or completions. Select the one that BEST answers the question or completes the statement. *PRINT THE LETTER OF THE CORRECT ANSWER IN THE SPACE AT THE RIGHT.*

1. If the crank shown in the sketch is rotated 360 degrees, then the piston will come to rest at position
    A. w
    B. x
    C. y
    D. z

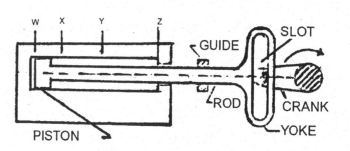

1.____

2. In the sketch shown, the volume of the bar, in cubic inches, is
    A. 32
    B. 48
    C. 60
    D. 96

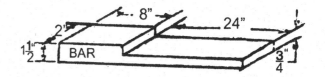

2.____

3. In the sketch, the ARM is exactly balanced as shown. If nut X is removed entirely, then in order to rebalance the ARM, it will be NECESSARY to move nut
    A. Y upward
    B. Y downward
    C. Z toward the left
    D. Z toward the right

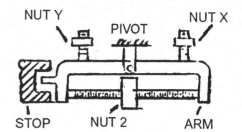

3.____

4. If the area of the movable diaphragm in the sketch is 6 square inches, then the air pressure required to balance the dead weight exactly, in pounds per square inch, is
    A. 9
    B. 12
    C. 15
    D. 18

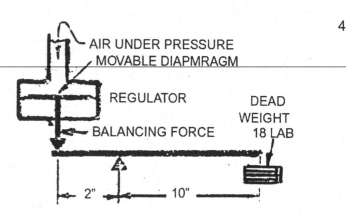

4.____

5. The sketch shows a non-slipping friction drive mechanism.
In order to rotate the driven wheel one complete revolution, it is NECESSARY to rotate the driving wheel through an angle of

5.____

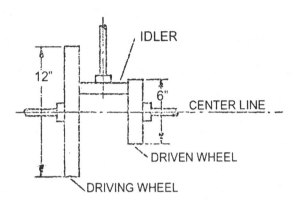

A. 90°
B. 180°
C. 270°
D. 360°

6. All 4 springs shown in the sketch are identical. In comparing the total stretch X in Case 1 with the total stretch J in Case 2, the total stretch X is MOST NEARLY _____ Y.

6.____

A. one-half of
B. equal to
C. two times
D. four times

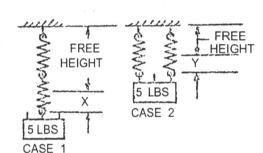

7. If the cam, shown in the sketch, is rotating at 60 RPM, then the contacts will come together once every

7.____

A. four seconds
B. two seconds
C. second
D. half-second

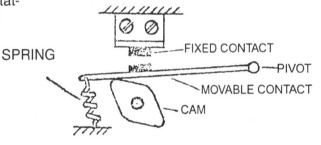

8. If both springs shown in the sketch are identical, then the *relative* tension in the springs is such that the tension in spring #1 is _____ the tension in #2.

8.____

A. one-quarter of
B. one-half of
C. equal to
D. twice

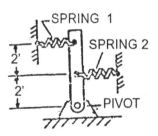

9. The sketch shows the reading which was recorded from a turnstile passenger counter at 8:00 A.M. If 10,000 passengers pass through this turnstile during the next 8 hour period, then, at 4:00 P.M., the counter should read

9.____

A. 415363
B. 416263
C. 425263
D. 515263

10. If the screw piston of the dead weight tester shown in the sketch is screwed downward, the
    A. plunger will be lowered
    B. plunger will be raised
    C. gage reading will increase
    D. gage reading will decrease

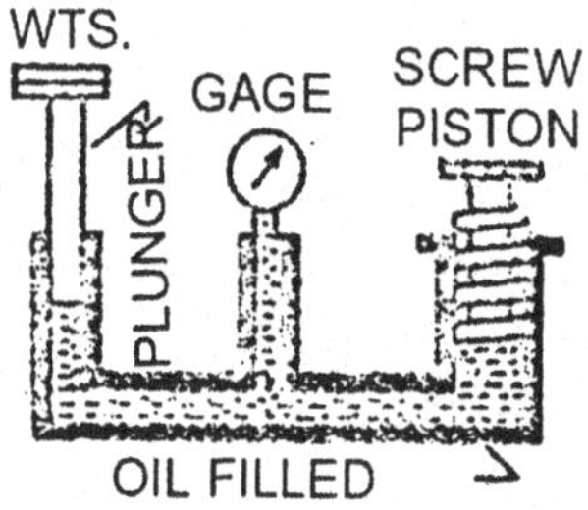

10.____

11. The larger roller in the sketch is 1" in diameter and the smaller roller is 1/2" in diameter. If the frame is moved to the left so that the larger roller rotates through one revolution, then the number of revolutions the smaller roller will rotate is
    A. 1/2
    B. 1
    C. 2
    D. 4

11.____

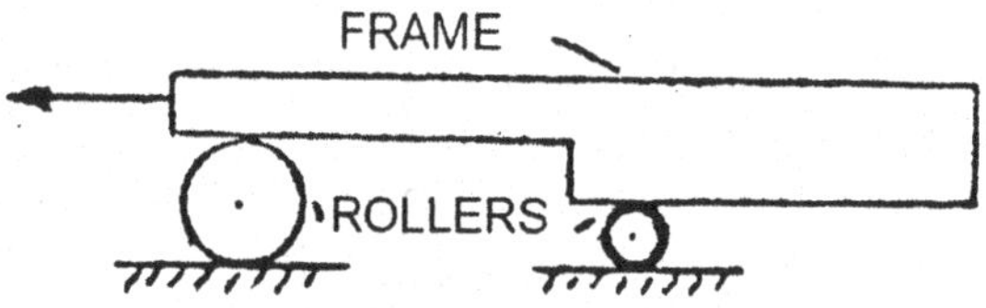

12. To bring the level of the fluid in the tanks shown in the sketch to a height of 1 1/2', the quantity of fluid to be added, in quarts, is MOST NEARLY
    A. 5
    B. 10
    C. 20
    D. 30

12.____

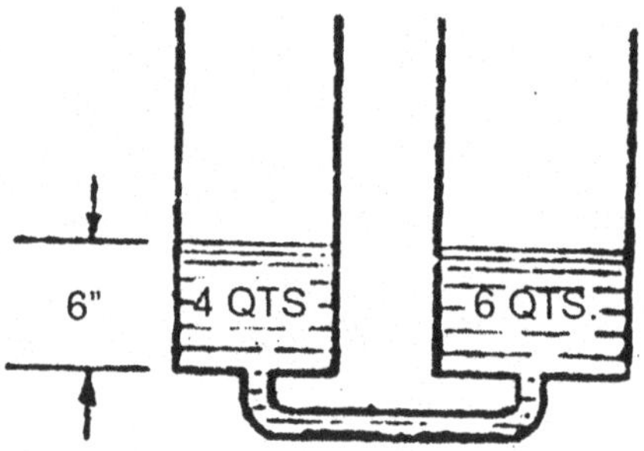

13. A type of hardware which can be used to make temporary electrical connections when testing an electrical circuit or component is a(n)

    A. Dzus fastener   B. cable clamp
    C. nylon clip   D. alligator clip

13.____

14. The spring shown in the sketch is a _____ spring.
    A. tension
    B. compression
    C. cantilever leaf
    D. torsion

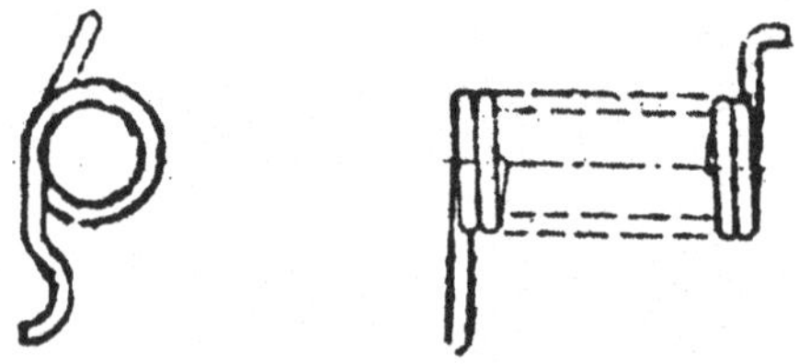

14.____

15. In order to open the valve shown in the sketch once every second, the wheel MUST rotate at _____ RPM.

     A. 1
     B. 6
     C. 10
     D. 20

15. ____

16. If the belt shown in the sketch is shifted to the left, then the spindle

     A. RPM will increase
     B. RPM will decrease
     C. RPM will remain the same
     D. rotation will reverse direction

16. ____

17. The threaded block shown in the sketch can slide in the slot but cannot revolve.
    If the hand-wheel is turned 10 revolutions clockwise, the threaded block will move _____ inch to the

     A. 1/2; left
     B. 1/2; right
     C. 1; left
     D. 1; right

17. ____

18. One complete revolution of the windless drum, shown in the sketch, will move the weight up

     A. 6"
     B. 9"
     C. 12"
     D. 36"

18. ____

19. If the pulley marked Y in in the double belt drive shown is revolving at 400 RPM, then the speed of pulley X is _____ RPM.

     A. 100
     B. 400
     C. 200
     D. 800

19. ____

20. If the worm gear shown in the sketch is rotated on revolution, then the sector gear will rotate through an angle of

    A. 5°
    B. 10°
    C. 20°
    D. 40°

20.____

SINGLE THREAD WORM GEAR

20°

SECTOR BEAR

21. The sketch shows an assembly, the parts of which have been labeled and given numbers.
    Of the following procedures, the one which describes the CORRECT order of assembly is

    A. 2 into 1; 5 thru 3; 4 thru 3 and 5; 3 and 5 into 1; and 5 into 2
    B. 4 thru 3; 5 into 2; 3 over 5; and 5, 3, and 2 into 1
    C. 5 thru 3; 4 thru 3 and 5; 5 into 2; and 5, 3, and 2 into 1
    D. 5 thru 3; 5 into 2; 5, 3, and 2 into 1; and 4 thru 3 and 5

21.____

ROD 5 WITH COLLAR AND THREADED END

CYLINDER 1 (OPEN AT THE END ONLY)

SCREW - CAP 2

TAPER PIN 4

ROD 5

BUSHING 3

22. Assume that you are a maintainer working in a certain work area and you observe a *live* wire which has fallen to the floor.
    You should

    A. immediately close off the area and then notify your supervisor
    B. take no action as this is not part of your duties
    C. notify the station supervisor next time you see him
    D. call the fire department

22.____

23. When tools in a repair shop are found in poor condition, the cause of this condition is MOST often that the tools have

    A. been improperly designed
    B. been used improperly
    C. never been used before
    D. been stored in a locked room

23.____

24. The type of fire extinguishing material that you should NOT use to extinguish a fire around electrical circuits is

    A. water
    C. dry chemical
    B. dry sand
    D. carbon dioxide

24.____

25. If a maintainer does not understand a new procedure which has been explained by his foreman, he SHOULD

    A. refuse to follow the new procedure
    B. ask for a different assignment
    C. follow the procedure used on previous jobs
    D. ask the foreman to explain it to him again

25.____

26. When lifting a heavy object, a man should NOT   26.____

    A. bend his knees
    B. have solid footing
    C. twist his body
    D. take a firm grip on the object

27. Of the following factors, the one that is MOST likely to be the cause of frequent accidents   27.____
in heavy machinery repair shops is that

    A. materials are left on the floor instead of in designated storage areas
    B. critical parts are kept locked in storage areas
    C. certain tools are overhauled instead of being replaced yearly
    D. emergencies frequently require changes in work schedules

Questions 28-33.

DIRECTIONS: Questions 28 through 33, inclusive, are based SOLELY on the information
contained in the passage given below.

INSTRUCTIONS ON HOW TO OPERATE AND MAINTAIN MODEL X COIN COUNTER

The machine is shipped completely assembled except for the crank handle which is detached. To place the crank in position, the maintainer inserts the crank handle and tightens the screw. As this machine counts all denominations of coin, it is necessary to set both the thickness gage and the width gage for the size coin to be counted.

To set the thickness gage, the maintainer turns the knob until the desired coin figure lines up with the index pointer. When the coins are worn thin, a closer setting of the thickness gage may be necessary.

To set the width gage, the maintainer unscrews the know about a half-turn, then slides the plate until the desired coin figures line up, then tightens the knob.

The lock count mechanism is used to lock the machine after counting 20 quarters or halves, 40 nickels or quarters, 50 pennies or dimes. To set the lock count, the maintainer raises the trip lever and moves the lock index knob until the pointer is opposite the proper notch. He moves the lock index knob all the way forward for a continuous count. (When using continuous count, the machines does not lock.)

To count into bags, the maintainer sets the thickness gage and the width gage for the type of coin to be counted, then he sets the continous count knob, and fastens the bag over the hooks on the stem.

To count and package, the maintainer places the crimper bracket in position by pushing the two pins as far as they will go into the holes in the front edge of the base of the machine. He replaces the bagging stem with the proper size packaging stem. He sets the *look count* pin in the proper notch (40 for nickels or quarters, 50 for pennies or dimes). The machine is now set for counting and wrapping.

28. According to the above passage, when setting the width gage,　28.＿＿＿

    A. the maintainer slides a plate until the desired coin figures line up
    B. the maintainer turns the knob until the desired coin figures line up with the index pointer
    C. a closer setting of the thickness gage may be necessary
    D. the maintainer clamps the knob with a locking set screw

29. This machine is set to identify the denomination of coin to be counted by　29.＿＿＿

    A. making a weight measurement
    B. making an analysis of the material
    C. gaging both the width and thickness
    D. locking the index knob

30. This machine is capable of counting　30.＿＿＿

    A. only pennies and dimes
    B. only nickels and quarters
    C. only quarters and halves
    D. all denominations of coin

31. The thickness gage is set by lining up the　31.＿＿＿

    A. desired coin figure with width plate
    B. desired coin figure with index pointer
    C. knob with trip lever
    D. knob with crank handle

32. The only piece which is NOT already attached to the machine when it is shipped is the　32.＿＿＿

    A. thickness gage   B. lock index knob
    C. crank handle   D. width gage

33. The lock count mechanism can be set to lock the machine after counting　33.＿＿＿

    A. 10 quarters or halves   B. 20 nickels or quarters
    C. 50 pennies or dimes   D. 100 dollar bills

34. Metal enclosures and panels that house electrical equipment should be grounded in order to　34.＿＿＿

    A. reduce shock hazard
    B. prevent short circuits
    C. simplify wiring layouts
    D. prevent electrolytic corrosion

35. Goggles should be worn while　35.＿＿＿

    A. setting up a milling machine
    B. oiling precision machinery
    C. filing a cam by hand
    D. grinding a cold chisel

36. In a turnstile mechanism, it is required that a clearance of .015" - .018" be maintained   36.____
    between a cam and its follower, measured at the low point of the cam.
    The instrument that should be used to measure this clearance ACCURATELY is a

    A. telescopic gage   B. depth micrometer
    C. set of feeler gages   D. inside vernier caliper

37. A material which is COMMONLY used for forming small diameter compression springs is   37.____
    _____ wire.

    A. aluminum
    B. annealed copper
    C. galvanized annealed steel
    D. hard-drawn steel

38. Movable electrical contacts attached to a bimetallic spring might GENERALLY be found   38.____
    in a(n)

    A. cartridge fuse
    B. electronic circuit breaker
    C. magnetic circuit breaker
    D. thermal circuit breaker

39. Assume that you have been assigned to maintain and evaluate a group of new turnstiles   39.____
    which have been installed in a station. You find that a certain brass bushing, designed for
    easy field replacement, has been wearing out rapidly causing erratic operation of all the
    machines.
    In your report to your supervisor, you should

    A. make no recommendation since this is the manufacturer's problem alone
    B. recommend that the stock of brass bushings be returned to the manufacturer
    C. recommend that the bushings be replaced with test bushings made of a harder
        material
    D. recommend that the machines be removed to the shop for this repair

40. The BEST way to determine which wire of a two-wire 120-volt A.C. line is the   40.____
    ungrounded wire is to

    A. quickly ground each line in turn
    B. test with one finger on the wire and one finger to ground
    C. determine the polarity by connecting a voltmeter across the line
    D. connect one lead of a test lamp to the conduit, and test with the other

KEY (CORRECT ANSWERS)

1.	A	11.	C	21.	C	31.	B
2.	C	12.	C	22.	A	32.	C
3.	D	13.	D	23.	B	33.	C
4.	C	14.	D	24.	A	34.	A
5.	D	15.	B	25.	D	35.	D
6.	D	16.	B	26.	C	36.	C
7.	D	17.	A	27.	A	37.	D
8.	B	18.	C	28.	A	38.	D
9.	C	19.	A	29.	C	39.	C
10.	B	20.	B	30.	D	40.	D

EXAMINATION SECTION
TEST 1

DIRECTIONS: Each question or incomplete statement is followed by several suggested answers or completions. Select the one that BEST answers the question or completes the statement. *PRINT THE LETTER OF THE CORRECT ANSWER IN THE SPACE AT THE RIGHT.*

1. Two lamps need 50V and 2 amp each in order to operate at a desired brilliancy. If they are to be connected in series across a 120V line, the resistance, in ohms, of the rheostat that must be placed in series with the lamps needs to be

    A. 4   B. 10   C. 20   D. 100   1._____

2. The Kelvin Bridge is BASICALLY a device for measuring   2._____

    A. low resistance   B. high resistance
    C. high emf   D. low emf

3. If a capacitance of 250 Mf, connected to an AC line, has a capacitive reactance measured at 10.6 ohms, the AC line has a frequency, in c/sec, of

    A. 30   B. 60   C. 90   D. 120   3._____

4. Of the following, the one that is NOT normally used as a component of some electronic oscillator circuits is the   4._____

    A. lighthouse tube   B. pitot tube
    C. klystron   D. magnetron

5. The term *magnetostriction* refers to the   5._____

    A. strict conditions that determine magnetic polarity
    B. change in dimensions when a substance is magnetized
    C. Curie point
    D. magnetic properties near absolute zero

6. In a three-phase alternator, the armature is Y-connected and three terminals are brought out.
If the voltage per armature phase is 200V, the line voltage is CLOSEST to which one of the following?   6._____

    A. 140V   B. 170V   C. 340V   D. 400V

7. If a charged capacitor loses one-half its charge by leakage, it has lost what fraction of its store of energy?   7._____

    A. 1/8   B. 1/4   C. 1/2   D. 3/4

8. An electrical current flows through an iron wire connected in series with another iron wire of equal length but one-half its cross-section area.
If the voltage drop across the thicker wire is 8 volts, the drop across the thinner wire, in volts, is CLOSEST to   8._____

    A. 2   B. 4   C. 8   D. 16

9. Of the following connections, the one which may be used to convert a galvanometer into a voltmeter is that of a _____-ohm resistor in _____.   9.____

    A. .005; series   B. .005; parallel
    C. 5000; series   D. 5000; parallel

10. A pivoted compass needle placed directly beneath a horizontal wire carrying an electrical current will orient itself so that its   10.____

    A. long axis is parallel to the wire
    B. long axis is perpendicular to the wire
    C. north pole will point downward
    D. north pole will point upward

11. The element of an n-p-n transistor which is analogous to the grid of a vacuum tube is the   11.____

    A. base   B. collector
    C. emitter   D. suppressor

12. An example of a transducer is a   12.____

    A. transistor   B. telephone transmitter
    C. transformer   D. thermonionic tube

13. In a parallel electrical circuit, the device with the LOWEST resistance has the   13.____

    A. least heating effect   B. highest wattage
    C. lowest current   D. lowest voltage drop

14. A device known as a transducer is used to convert   14.____

    A. AC to DC and back again
    B. a light beam into sound
    C. heat waves into sound pressure and back again
    D. sound pressure to electric signals and back again

15. Two resistances of 6 and 24 ohms are connected in series to a 120-volt source. The voltage drop across the 6 ohm resistor is   15.____

    A. 4   B. 18   C. 24   D. 96

16. Four capacitors, each of 10 microfarads capacity, are fully charged when connected in parallel.
The TOTAL equivalent capacity of this combination, in microfarads, is   16.____

    A. 2.5   B. 10   C. 14   D. 40

17. The peak voltage of an alternating emf is 141 volts. The EFFECTIVE value of the voltage, in volts, is   17.____

    A. 70.5   B. 100   C. 141   D. 200

18. In a step-down transformer, the secondary winding is usually thicker than the primary winding because the secondary has the HIGHER   18.____

    A. current   B. wattage
    C. voltage   D. resistance

19. A 100-watt lamp is able to generate more light and heat than a 60-watt lamp because the 100-watt lamp

    A. draws less current
    B. is usually operated at a higher voltage
    C. usually uses a different filament material
    D. has less resistance

19.____

20. Three ideal components: a resistor, an inductor, and a capacitor, are connected in series to a source of AC. The potential difference across each component is 40 volts. The TOTAL voltage across the three components is

    A. zero   B. $40\sqrt{2}V$ C. 40V   D. 120V

20.____

21. The potential difference across a 6-ohm resistor is 6 volts. The power used by the resistor is, in watts,

    A. 6   B. 12   C. 18   D. 24

21.____

22. In a sinusoidal alternating current, the peak value of the current equals

    A. the effective value of the current
    B. 0.707 times the effective value of the current
    C. 1.41 times the effective value of the current
    D. 0.707 times the peak value of the emf divided by the resistance

22.____

23. Electrical resistance is equivalent to which one of the following?

    A. Work/charge   B. Work • time/charge
    C. Work • time/charge^2 D. Work • time/current

23.____

24. At 60 cycles per second, a coil has an inductive reactance of 100 ohms and a certain capacitor has a capacitive reactance of 400 ohms. At what frequency, in cy/sec, will the two devices have the SAME reactance?

    A. 30   B. 120   C. 180   D. 240

24.____

25. Which one of the following purposes may be served by a diode in a vacuum tube circuit?

    A. Amplifier   B. Condenser
    C. Resistor   D. Detector

25.____

26. In a series-wound motor, the current present in the armature winding is _____ is applied to the motor.

    A. DC even when AC   B. DC when DC
    C. AC only when AC   D. AC even when DC

26.____

27. The electromotive force, in volts, of 4 fresh similar dry cells, connected in parallel, is usually CLOSEST to which one of the following?

    A. 1.5   B. 3   C. 4.5   D. 6

27.____

28. An alternating current generator differs from a direct current generator by having

    A. splip-rings   B. brushes
    C. a split-ring commutator   D. an armature

28.____

29. The GREATEST number of 100 watt lamps which can be connected in parallel in a 120 volt system without blowing a 10 ampere fuse is   29.____

    A. 12   B. 18   C. 24   D. 30

30. The construction of a direct current motor is basically the SAME as that of a(n)   30.____

    A. direct current generator
    B. alternating current motor
    C. alternating current generator
    D. ballistic galvanometer

31. A galvanometer may be used as an ammeter by   31.____

    A. shunting the galvanometer with a high resistance
    B. connecting a low resistance in parallel with the galvanometer
    C. connecting a low resistance in series
    D. connecting a high resistance in series

32. Resistances of 20 ohms and 60 ohms are connected in parallel to a generator. If the current in the 60 ohm resistance is 1 ampere, the current in the 20 ohm resistance will be _____ ampere(s).   32.____

    A. 1   B. 1/3   C. 2/3   D. 3

33. Direct current may be changed to alternating current by the use of a   33.____

    A. transformer   B. rectifier
    C. spark coil   D. diode

34. Iron and copper wires of equal lengths and cross-sections are connected in series. During the passage of current through the wires for a period of two minutes, the   34.____

    A. voltage drop across the copper will be larger than across the iron
    B. current through the copper will be greater than that through the iron
    C. current through the iron will be greater than that through the copper
    D. heat generated in the iron will be greater than that in the copper

35. If the current flowing through a given resistor is doubled, the amount of heat generated is multiplied by   35.____

    A. 1/2   B. 1   C. 2   D. 4

36. In wiring an electrical circuit, the laboratory assistant should make the *live* connection the _____ act in assembling and the _____ act in disassembling.   36.____

    A. last; first   B. first; first
    C. last; last   D. first; last

37. The electric current used in the school laboratory should be   37.____

    A. alternating and not direct
    B. direct and not alternating
    C. below 20 volts
    D. sent through a limiting load resistance

38. Which one of the following pairs of factors determines the direction of an induced electro-   38.____
motive force?
Direction of

    A. motion and direction of field
    B. motion and rate of rotation
    C. field and rate of rotation
    D. field and number of turns on coil

39. A rectifier is a device used to   39.____

    A. change direct current into alternating current
    B. increase the voltage
    C. filter out stray currents
    D. change alternating current to direct current

40. When a small quantity of a gas like mercury vapor is introduced into a diode, its net effect   40.____
is to do which one of the following?

    A. Reduce plate current flow
    B. Increase the number of negative ions
    C. Increase the number of electrons reaching the plate
    D. Decrease the number of positive ions

41. The capacitive reactance of a circuit is increased by which one of the following?   41.____
A(n)

    A. increase in the frequency of the voltage
    B. decrease in the frequency of the voltage
    C. increase in the resistance of the circuit
    D. decrease in the resistance of the circuit

42. In an electrical circuit containing both inductance and capacitance, if the capacitance   42.____
increases, the natural frequency of the circuit will

    A. increase
    B. decrease
    C. increase to a maximum then decrease
    D. remain constant

43. Of the following, the type of coupling in a radio circuit that is LEAST likely to introduce   43.____
distortion is

    A. resistance   B. transformer
    C. impedance   D. capacitive

44. The function of the grid in a triode is to   44.____

    A. supply electrons
    B. control the plate current
    C. control the temperature of the tube
    D. control the plate voltage

45. The ESSENTIAL difference between an audio and a radio frequency transformer is the absence in the radio transformer of a(n)   45.____

    A. capacitor   B. iron core
    C. quartz crystal   D. transistor element

46. The PRINCIPAL effect of the space charge in a vacuum tube is to   46.____

    A. decrease the plate current
    B. increase the plate current
    C. increase the plate voltage
    D. increase the electron emission from the cathode

47. In the expression for induced emf, $V = \dfrac{-d\varnothing}{dt}$, the minus sign is a consequence of _____ Law.   47.____

    A. Coulomb's   B. Biot-Savart
    C. Lenz's   D. Faraday's

48. An oscillating circuit contains an inductance of 10uh, a capacitor of 5uf, and a capacitor of 25uf, all in parallel. The natural frequency of the circuit, in kilocycles/sec, is CLOSEST to which one of the following?   48.____

    A. 4.7   B. 9.2   C. 4,700   D. 9,200

49. During normal operation, AC is present in which one of the following?   49.____

    A. Armature winding of a DC motor
    B. Field winding of a DC motor
    C. Field winding of a DC generator
    D. Coil of a ballistic galvanometer

50. The emission of electrons from the surface of a heated conductor was FIRST observed by   50.____

    A. Fleming   B. Hertz   C. Armstrong   D. Edison

KEY (CORRECT ANSWERS)

1.	B	11.	A	21.	A	31.	B	41.	B
2.	A	12.	B	22.	C	32.	D	42.	B
3.	B	13.	B	23.	C	33.	C	43.	A
4.	B	14.	D	24.	B	34.	D	44.	B
5.	B	15.	C	25.	D	35.	D	45.	B
6.	C	16.	D	26.	D	36.	A	46.	A
7.	D	17.	B	27.	A	37.	D	47.	C
8.	D	18.	A	28.	A	38.	A	48.	B
9.	C	19.	D	29.	A	39.	D	49.	A
10.	B	20.	C	30.	A	40.	C	50.	D

———

TEST 2

DIRECTIONS: Each question or incomplete statement is followed by several suggested answers or completions. Select the one that BEST answers the question or completes the statement. *PRINT THE LETTER OF THE CORRECT ANSWER IN THE SPACE AT THE RIGHT.*

1. Lenz's Law states that the   1._____

    A. induced current is always equal in magnitude to the impressed current
    B. induced field has a direction opposite to that of the original field if this is decreasing
    C. induced field always has such direction as to aid the motion of a conductor moving in the field
    D. induced field has the same direction as the original if this is decreasing

2. A long straight wire is in a magnetic field and, when the wire carries a current of 4 amp,   2._____
    the magnetic field exerts on it a force per unit length equal to K.
    If the current is changed to one amp and the magnetic flux density is doubled, the force per unit length is

    A. K/8   B. K/4   C. K/2   D. K

3. In an AC series circuit, the inductive reactance, capacitive reactance, and resistance are   3._____
    25 ohms each.
    When a 100 volt AC potential difference is applied, the current flow, in amperes, will equal

    A. 1.3   B. 4   C. 13   D. 2500

4. The plate current in an electron tube is initially 10 milliamperes under certain conditions.   4._____
    When the plate voltage is increased by 10 volts, the plate current becomes 11 milliam-
    peres. Under the same original conditions, an increase of grid voltage of 1 volt increases
    the plate current to 11 milliamperes.
    The amplification factor of the tube is then

    A. 0.1   B. 10   C. 100   D. 110

5. To obtain the HIGHEST possible transformer efficiency, it would be desirable to have the   5._____

    A. turn ratio as high as possible
    B. input current low and output current high
    C. core made of solid copper
    D. hysteresis loop as narrow as possible

6. If a capacitor, 10^{-4} farad capacity, and a 1 megohm resistor are connected in series to a   6._____
    100 volt battery, the time constant, in seconds, for this circuit is

    A. 10^{-2} B. 10^{-1} C. 10^2 D. 10^4

7. The impedance Z of an alternating current circuit is ALWAYS given by the formula Z =   7._____

    A. $2\pi fL$ B. $1/2\pi fC$

    C. $2\pi fL - 1/2\pi fC$ D. $\sqrt{R^2 + (2\pi fL - 1/2\pi fC)^2}$

8. The transmission of an electric current through an electrolyte is done by means of   8.____

    A. electrons *only*
    B. positive and negative ions
    C. positive ions *only*
    D. positive ions and electrons

9. Of the following, a device which is ALWAYS connected in parallel in a circuit is a(n)   9.____

    A. ammeter   B. fuse   C. switch   D. voltmeter

10. A diode may be used as which one of the following?   10.____

    A. Amplifier   B. Oscillator
    C. Rectifier   D. Transformer

11. In an n-p-n transistor used as an amplifier, which one of the following is a NECESSARY   11.____
connection?
_____ side of battery _____.

    A. Negative; A to emitter
    B. Negative; B to collector
    C. Negative; A to base
    D. Positive; B to base

12. When two 4 ohm resistors are joined in series and connected to a power supply which   12.____
consists of a 7 volt battery whose positive terminal is connected to that of a 9V battery,
the current flow in the resistors is, in amperes, the two free terminals being connected to
the resistors,

    A. 0.25   B. 1.0   C. 2.0   D. 8.0

13. A wattmeter, when properly connected in the circuit, is connected   13.____

    A. only in series
    B. only in parallel
    C. either in series or in parallel
    D. both in series and in parallel

14. When an incandescent lamp rated at 120V, 60W draws a current of 0.5 amp, the number   14.____
of electrons/sec passing through the wire is

    A. $(0.5)(6.25 \times 10^{18})$ B. $(0.5)(1.6 \times 10^{-19})$
    C. $(60)(0.5)(1.6 \times 10^{-19})$ D. $(60)(0.5)(6.25 \times 10^{18})$

15. When a resistor and a capacitor are connected in series to a dry cell, at the instant of   15.____
closing the circuit, the

    A. voltage across the resistor is zero
    B. voltage across the capacitor is at maximum
    C. charge on the capacitor is at maximum
    D. current in the circuit is at maximum

16. An electron and a proton are accelerated from rest through a potential difference of 1000   16.____
volts.
As a result, the ratio of the kinetic energy of the proton to that of the electron is

    A. 1:1   B. 1840:1   C. 1:1840   D. 1000:1

17. If a uniform wire 10 feet long having a resistance of 1.0 ohm is cut into 10 equal pieces   17.____
which are then connected in parallel with each other, the resistance of this parallel array,
expressed in ohms, is

    A. 0.010   B. 0.10   C. 1.0   D. 10

18. When a 30 volt, 60-cycle AC source is connected to a 90-ohm resistor in series with a 50   18.____
uf capacitor and a 60 millihenry inductance, the impedance of the circuit, in ohms, is
CLOSEST to which one of the following?

    A. 45   B. 70   C. 95   D. 120

19. When a 10 foot length of copper wire having a resistance of 2 ohms is drawn out, with   19.____
uniform thickness, to a length of 30 feet, its resistance, in ohms, will be which one of the
following?

    A. 2   B. 6   C. 12   D. 18

20. The force of attraction between two opposite electric charges is 24 dynes.   20.____
If the positive charge is doubled, and the negative charge is halved, the force of attraction will be

    A. halved   B. unchanged
    C. doubled   D. quadrupled

21. Wire A has a resistance of 1,000 ohms.   21.____
If wire B, which is of the same material as A and at the same temperature, is twice as
long as A and has a cross-sectional area 5 times that of A, the resistance of B, in
ohms, will be

    A. 100   B. 400   C. 2,500   D. 10,000

22. If a 1-HP electric motor draws 4 amp when operating from a 220-volt line, the efficiency   22.____
of the motor, in percent, is CLOSEST to which one of the following?

    A. 65   B. 75   C. 85   D. 95

23. Which one of the following represents, in ohms, the resistance of a 1,000-watt DC elec-   23.____
tric heater drawing a current of 10 amp?

    A. 10   B. 100   C. 900   D. 10,000

24. If a 30-volt, 60-cycle AC source is connected to a circuit containing in series a 90-ohm   24.____
resistor, a 50 uf capacitor, and a 60 millihenry inductance, the tangent of the phase angle
is CLOSEST to which one of the following?

    A. .17   B. .34   C. .51   D. .68

25. A circuit containing an inductance of 320 uh and a capacitance of 80 uuf will have a res- 25.____
onant frequency, in c/sec, CLOSEST to which one of the following?

    A. 60   B. 1×10^3 C. 1×10^4 D. 1×10^6

26. If an electric iron whose resistance is 24 ohms draws 5 amperes, what heat energy will 26.____
be produced, in joules, in one hour?

    A. 2.16×10^5 B. 5.18×10^5 C. 2.16×10^6 D. 5.18×10^6

27. A galvanometer having a resistance of 50 ohms reads full scale with a current of 1 milli- 27.____
ampere.
To convert the galvanometer to a 10-volt voltmeter requires a multiplier whose resistance, in ohms, is

    A. 9,500   B. 9,950   C. 10,000   D. 10,050

28. When three capacitors, 8, 10, and 40 uf, respectively, are connected in series to a 300- 28.____
volt DC source, the combined capacitance in the circuit, in uf, is CLOSEST to which one
of the following?

    A. 4   B. 5.14   C. 29   D. 58

29. In order for a 30-volt, 90-watt lamp to work properly when inserted in a 120-volt DC line, 29.____
it should have in series with it a resistor whose resistance, in ohms, is

    A. 10   B. 20   C. 30   D. 40

30. The combined resistance of two resistors (R_1 and R_2) in parallel is given by which one of 30.____
the following formulas?
$R_T=$

    A. $\dfrac{R_1 + R_2}{R_1 R_2}$ B. $\dfrac{R_1 R_2}{R_1 + R_2}$ C. $\dfrac{2R_1}{R_1 + R_2}$ D. $\dfrac{2R_2}{R_1 + R_2}$

31. If an ordinary dry cell delivers 30 amp when shortcircuited, which one of the following is 31.____
the internal resistance of the cell, in ohms?

    A. 0.033   B. 0.05   C. 0.066   D. 0.2

32. When a 60-watt, 120-volt incandescent lamp is connected in parallel with a 40-watt, 120- 32.____
volt lamp, the combined resistance of the lamps, in ohms, is CLOSEST to which one of
the following?

    A. 24   B. 144   C. 240   D. 360

33. The name plate on a certain motor gives the following information: 5hp, 230V, 18 33.____
amp,1200 rpm.
The efficiency of the motor should, therefore, be

    A. 80%   B. 85%   C. 90%   D. 95%

34. In an AC series circuit, there is an inductive reactance of 20 ohms, a capacitive reac-   34.____
tance of 10 ohms, and a resistance of 5 ohms.
The impedance to current flow, in ohms, in this circuit will be CLOSEST to which one
of the following?

   A. 6   B. 11   C. 15   D. 35

35. When an inductance coil of 2.5 henrys is tuned to resonate at 100 cycles/sec, the capac-   35.____
itor should have a magnitude, in microfarads, CLOSEST to which one of the following?

   A. 0.5   B. 1.0   C. 10.0   D. 100.0

36. When a resistor, a coil, and a capacitor are connected in series to an AC generator, the   36.____
current through the capacitor must be in phase with the voltage across the

   A. resistor   B. coil
   C. capacitor   D. whole circuit

37. If two adjacent parallel conductors free to move are placed within 1 cm of each other, and   37.____
a 20 ampere direct current is sent through each in the same direction, the tendency of
the conductors will be to

   A. move apart
   B. remain stationary
   C. come together
   D. rotate in either a clockwise or counter-clockwise direction

38. An electron beam is moving from left to right in a cathode ray tube.   38.____
When a strong S pole is placed above the beam, the electron beam will be deflected

   A. toward the observer   B. vertically upward
   C. away from the observer   D. vertically downward

39. When a pear-shaped metallic shell is charged positively, the potential of the more   39.____
pointed end is

   A. less than that of the opposite end
   B. greater than that of the opposite end
   C. the same as that of the opposite end
   D. less than that of the adjacent surface

40. When a parallel-plate capacitor is kept connected to a battery of constant emf, and the   40.____
plates of the capacitor are moved further apart by the use of insulated handles, which
one of the following occurs?
The

   A. capacitance increases
   B. capacitance remains the same
   C. charge on the capacitor remains the same
   D. charge on the capacitor decreases

41. Voltage may be correctly expressed in which one of the following ways?   41.____

   A. Coulombs/elementary charge
   B. Coulombs/sec

C. Dynes/cm
D. Joules/elementary charge

42. In the half-wave power supply, the filter capacitor does which one of the following?   42.____
   It

   A. increases input voltage variation
   B. increases maximum voltage output
   C. reduces output voltage variation
   D. limits the input voltage

43. The term *effective current,* as used in sinusoidal AC circuits, means the SAME as the   43.____
   term _____ current.

   A. average   B. root-mean-square
   C. peak   D. instantaneous

44. When an AC generator produces its peak voltage of 160V, the instantaneous current   44.____
   flow, in amperes, in a 20 ohm resistance connected to it will be

   A. 4   B. 5.7   C. 8   D. 28.2

45. Of the following, the material with the HIGHEST resistivity is   45.____

   A. silver   B. copper   C. aluminum   D. nichrome

46. A 0-10 milliampere meter has a resistance of 20 ohms.   46.____
   To convert this meter to an ammeter with a range of 0-1 ampere, we should connect a
   resistance of

   A. approximately 2000 ohms in series
   B. approximately 2000 ohms in parallel
   C. 200 ohms in series
   D. 1/5 ohm in parallel

47. A 60 watt lamp and a 600 watt toaster are operating in parallel on a 120 volt circuit.   47.____
   The resistance ratio of lamp to toaster is

   A. 1/100   B. 1/10   C. 10/1   D. 100/1

48. When the secondary circuit of a transformer is completed, the current in the primary   48.____

   A. decreases
   B. remains the same
   C. increases
   D. increases or decreases, depending on the ratio of turns

49. The phase angle in an alternating current circuit is zero degrees when the circuit   49.____

   A. contains resistance *only*
   B. contains inductance *only*
   C. contains capacitance *only*
   D. is not closed

50. When a capacitor of 10 microfarads capacity is connected to a 100 volt current source, the charge acquired by the capacitor will have a magnitude, in coulombs, of   50.____

   A. 10^{-6} B. 10^{-4} C. 10^{2} D. 10^{3}

___

KEY (CORRECT ANSWERS)

1.	D	11.	A	21.	B	31.	B	41.	D
2.	C	12.	A	22.	C	32.	B	42.	C
3.	B	13.	D	23.	A	33.	C	43.	B
4.	B	14.	A	24.	B	34.	B	44.	C
5.	D	15.	D	25.	D	35.	B	45.	D
6.	C	16.	A	26.	C	36.	A	46.	D
7.	D	17.	A	27.	B	37.	C	47.	C
8.	B	18.	C	28.	A	38.	C	48.	C
9.	D	19.	D	29.	C	39.	C	49.	A
10.	C	20.	B	30.	B	40.	D	50.	B

EXAMINATION SECTION
TEST 1

DIRECTIONS: Each question or incomplete statement is followed by several suggested answers or completions. Select the one that BEST answers the question or completes the statement. *PRINT THE LETTER OF THE CORRECT ANSWER IN THE SPACE AT THE RIGHT.*

1. If a nichrome wire 2 meters long has a resistance of 10 ohms, the resistance of another nichrome wire 1 meter long and with a cross-sectional area half that of the longer wire is, in ohms,

    A. 5   B. 10   C. 20   D. 40

1.____

2. Two nichrome wires of exactly the same composition have the same weight, but one is 5 times as long as the other. If the resistance of the shorter wire is R, the resistance of the other is

    A. R   B. 5R   C. 25R   D. 50R

2.____

3. A magnet pole has a strength of 400 units.
The magnetic field intensity in air due to this pole and at a distance 4 cm from this pole is _____ oersteds.

    A. 25   B. 50   C. 100   D. 25π

3.____

4. The number of revolutions per minute that a 6-pole alternator must make to produce a frequency of 60 cycles/sec is

    A. 1080   B. 1200   C. 2160   D. 21,600

4.____

5. A voltmeter having a full scale deflection of 10 volts has an internal resistance of 1000 ohms.
To convert this instrument to a voltmeter having a full scale deflection of 300 volts requires, in ohms, a multiplier of

    A. 3000   B. 6000   C. 9000   D. 12,000

5.____

6. Which one of the following scientists is NOT directly connected with the invention and development of the transistor?

    A. John Bardeen   B. William B. Shockley
    C. Polykarp Kusch   D. Walter H. Brattain

6.____

7. If there is a current of 0.1 ampere through a lamp for 100 seconds, the number of coulombs passing through in that time is

    A. 0.1   B. 1   C. 10   D. 100

7.____

8. If the core of an electromagnet is made of 2 pieces of iron, each running the full length of the electromagnet, when a direct current is sent through the coil, the 2 core pieces will

    A. attract each other
    B. repel each other
    C. attract and repel alternately
    D. have no effect on each other

8.____

9. If a 25-watt, 120-volt lamp and a 100-watt, 12-volt lamp are connected in a series to a 120-volt source,   9.____

    A. both lamps light normally
    B. neither lamp lights
    C. the 100-watt lamp is brighter
    D. the 25-watt lamp is brighter

10. A 30-watt, 120-volt resistor is connected to a 120-volt, 60-cycle source.   10.____
The maximum current flow in the lamp, in amperes, is APPROXIMATELY

    A. 0.18   B. 0.25   C. 0.35   D. 0.4

11. A 0-20 milliampere meter has a resistance of 20 ohms. To convert this meter to a voltme-   11.____
ter with a range of 0-10 volts, one should connect a resistance of APPROXIMATELY
_____ ohms in _____.

    A. 200; series   B. 200; parallel
    C. 500; series   D. 500; parallel

12. The current flow through a galvanometer is 10^{-5} milliamperes and produces a deflection   12.____
of 1 scale division. If the resistance of the moving coil is 200 ohms, the voltage across
the coil, in volts, is

    A. 2×10^{-3} B. 5×10^{-10} C. 5×10^{-5} D. 2×10^{-6}

13. A capacitor using a dielectric whose coefficient is 5 has a capacitance of A.   13.____
An identical capacitor using a dielectric whose coefficient is 20 will have a capacitance
equal to

    A. 2A   B. 4A   C. 10A   D. 100A

14. When resonance occurs in a circuit supplied with an alternating voltage, the   14.____

    A. impedance equals zero
    B. inductance equals the reciprocal of the capacitance
    C. capacitance equals the inductance
    D. inductive reactance equals the capacitive reactance

15. An electric heating coil of 6 ohms resistance is connected across a 120-volt line for 10   15.____
minutes.
The energy liberated, in joules, in this period of time equals

    A. 7.2×10^3 B. 14.4×10^5
    C. 25.8×10^4 D. 43.2×10^4

16. If a triode has its plate current increased 20 milliamperes when the plate voltage is   16.____
increased from 50 to 90 volts and the plate current is also increased 20 milliamperes
when the grid potential changes 4 volts, the amplification factor of the tube is

    A. 1.8   B. 5.0   C. 10.0   D. 40.0

17. A charge of 30 coulombs passes through a wire in 3 seconds. The current flow in this   17.____
wire, in amperes, equals

    A. 3.3   B. 10   C. 30   D. 90

18. The heat developed by 5 amperes flowing through a resistance of 4 ohms is 18.____

    A. 20 calories   B. 24 calories per second
    C. 100 calories   D. 4.8 calories per degree

19. 1 e.s.u. of potential difference equals 19.____

    A. 1 volt   B. 300 joules/coulomb
    C. 10^8 e.m.u. of potential   D. 4.187 volts

20. Two electrical condensers having capacitances of 6 and 12 microfarads, respectively, are 20.____
connected in series. The TOTAL capacitance, in microfarads, of this combination is

    A. 2   B. 4   C. 9   D. 18

21. The voltage induced in a coil with an inductance of 0.25 henries when the current 21.____
decreased uniformly from 2 amperes to zero amperes in 1/16 second is

    A. 4   B. 8   C. 16   D. 24

22. A transformer placed on DC is LIKELY to burn out because of the absence of 22.____

    A. a fuse   B. voltage regulation
    C. hysteresis   D. inductive reactance

23. If the effective AC voltage of a given circuit is 100, the maximum voltage is CLOSEST to 23.____
which one of the following?

    A. 0   B. 71   C. 141   D. 173

24. One milliampere produces full scale deflection in a galvanometer whose internal resis- 24.____
tance is 50 ohms.
To convert this instrument into an ammeter whose full scale deflection is 1 amp, it
should be shunted with a resistance, in ohms, CLOSEST to which one of the following?

    A. 0.005   B. 0.05   C. 0.5   D. 5.0

25. The results of the Millikan oil drop experiment lead to the conclusion that 25.____

    A. electric charges are negative
    B. electric charges are due to a transfer of electrons
    C. there is a fundamental unit of charge
    D. there are no isolated magnetic poles

26. A 60-watt, 120-volt incandescent lamp has a resistance, in ohms, of 26.____

    A. 0.5   B. 2.0   C. 60   D. 240

27. A 0-5 amp ammeter reads full scale when its 2-ohm movable coil has a voltage of 0.01 27.____
applied across it.
The shunt has a resistance, in ohms, CLOSEST to which one of the following?

    A. 0.001   B. 0.002   C. 250   D. 500

28. The heat in kilocalories (1 kilocalorie = 4200 joules) developed by a 60 watt lamp in one 28.____
hour is APPROXIMATELY

    A. 36   B. 50   C. 60   D. 95

29. Assume that a circuit consisting of a coil and a capacitor is adjusted to give resonance.   29.____
If some turns are removed from the coil, then resonance can be restored by

    A. increasing the frequency
    B. decreasing the capacitance
    C. decreasing the frequency
    D. decreasing the inductance

30. A series AC circuit contains a resistance of 40 ohms, an inductive reactance of 100   30.____
ohms, and a capacitive reactance of 70 ohms.
The impedance of this circuit is, in ohms,

    A. 50   B. 110   C. 150   D. 210

31. A series AC circuit contains a 20-ohm resistance, a 40-ohm resistance, a 60-ohm induc-   31.____
tive reactance, and an 80-ohm capacitive reactance.
The GREATEST amount of heat per second produced by any of these will be produced by the

    A. 20-ohm resistance   B. 40-ohm resistance
    C. 60-ohm reactance   D. 80-ohm reactance

32. If a sheet of glass is slipped between the plates of an air capacitor, the capacitance of the   32.____
combination

    A. drops to zero
    B. is reduced to approximately one-half of the original value
    C. increases
    D. has a value which depends on the charge of the capacitor

33. The resistance of a piece of wire is 16 ohms.   33.____
The resistance, in ohms, of a piece of the same wire twice as long and twice the diameter is

    A. 8   B. 16   C. 32   D. 64

34. A circuit containing resistance, capacitance, and inductance is in resonance when sup-   34.____
plied with an alternating current of a given frequency.
An increase in the frequency of this current will

    A. decrease the inductive reactance
    B. increase the capacitive reactance
    C. increase the total current in the circuit
    D. decrease the impedance

35. The heat developed by a 5 ampere current flowing through a resistance of 4 ohms is   35.____

    A. 20 calories   B. 24 calories/sec
    C. 100 calories   D. 4.8 calories per degree

36. A capacitor stores 50 joules of energy when charged by a 5000 volt source.   36.____
The capacitance of the capacitor, in microfarads, is

    A. .02   B. .04   C. 2.0   D. 4.0

37. The amplification factor of a triode is represented BEST by which one of the following expressions?
The

    A. change in grid voltage divided by the change in filament voltage
    B. plate current
    C. change in plate voltage divided by the change in grid voltage needed to produce that change in plate current
    D. change in plate voltage divided by the change in plate current needed to produce that change in grid voltage

37._____

38. Kirchhoff's Laws with regard to the current in an electrical circuit states that

    A. current is directly proportional to voltage
    B. the algebraic sum of the currents at a junction equals zero
    C. current is inversely proportional to electrical resistance
    D. the total current in a parallel circuit equals the sum of the currents in the individual parallel branches

38._____

39. A Fleming valve or diode performs which one of the following functions?

    A. Converts rectified DC to AC
    B. Converts AC to half-wave rectified DC
    C. Converts AC to smooth DC
    D. Steps up low voltage AC to high voltage AC

39._____

40. A capacitor discharges at a certain frequency through a circuit containing an inductance. If the capacitance is multiplied by four, the oscillation frequency is multiplied by

    A. $\dfrac{1}{4}$ B. $\dfrac{1}{2}$ C. 2   D. 4

40._____

41. A coil of 100 turns is wound on an iron core. The coil is connected to an AC source. Suitable connections are made to display applied voltage and circuit current on an oscilloscope.
It is found that the current _____ the voltage by _____.

    A. leads; 90°   B. lags behind; 90°
    C. leads; an acute angle   D. lags behind; an acute angle

41._____

42. The mixing of an audio frequency electric current with a radio frequency carrier in a broadcasting station is known as

    A. oscillation   B. modulation
    C. amplification   D. rectification

42._____

43. An electron is accelerated through a potential difference of 20,000 volts. Its gain in kinetic energy is 20,000

    A. volts   B. joules
    C. electron volts   D. ergs

43._____

44. The radius of the circular path of a charged particle moving at right angles to a uniform magnetic field is DIRECTLY proportional to the

    44.____

    A. momentum of the particle
    B. flux density
    C. charge on the particle
    D. wavelength of its radiation

45. The direction of an induced current is always such that the magnetic field belonging to it tends to oppose the change in the strength of the magnetic field belonging to the primary current.
This law was FIRST enunciated by

    45.____

    A. Ampere   B. Faraday   C. Henry   D. Lenz

46. A split ring commutator will be found on a

    46.____

    A. synchronous motor
    B. AC generator
    C. DC motor
    D. induction-repulsion type of motor

47. A ballistic galvanometer is used MAINLY to measure which one of the following?

    47.____

    A. Electric charge   B. Electric current
    C. EMF   D. Resistance

48. If a calibrated oscilloscope shows a sinusoidal current having a peak to peak value of 2.0 amperes, the effective value of the current as measured by an ammeter and expressed in amperes would be

    48.____

    A. 0.50   B. 0.71   C. 1.0   D. 2.0

49. Of the following, the pair of functions of a vacuum tube that are MOST closely allied are

    49.____

    A. rectification and amplification
    B. oscillation and rectification
    C. amplification and detection
    D. detection and rectification

50. If a thin sheet of metal is placed halfway between the two plates of a parallel-plate, air-dielectric capacitor, the capacitance is

    50.____

    A. quadrupled
    B. doubled
    C. decreased to 1/2 of the original value
    D. decreased to 1/4

KEY (CORRECT ANSWERS)

1.	B	11.	C	21.	B	31.	B	41.	D
2.	C	12.	D	22.	D	32.	C	42.	B
3.	A	13.	B	23.	C	33.	A	43.	C
4.	B	14.	D	24.	B	34.	B	44.	A
5.	C	15.	B	25.	C	35.	B	45.	D
6.	C	16.	C	26.	D	36.	D	46.	C
7.	C	17.	B	27.	B	37.	C	47.	A
8.	B	18.	B	28.	B	38.	B	48.	B
9.	D	19.	B	29.	A	39.	B	49.	D
10.	C	20.	B	30.	A	40.	B	50.	C

TEST 2

DIRECTIONS: Each question or incomplete statement is followed by several suggested answers or completions. Select the one that BEST answers the question or completes the statement. *PRINT THE LETTER OF THE CORRECT ANSWER IN THE SPACE AT THE RIGHT.*

1. If a 1 mfd capacitor and a 2 mfd capacitor are connected in series across a 120-volt source, the potential difference across the 1 mfd capacitor is _____ volts.   1.____

    A. 30   B. 40   C. 60   D. 80

2. If a battery having an EMF of 6 volts and internal resistance of 0.6 ohms is supplying a current of 0.5 amperes, the terminal voltage is _____ volts.   2.____

    A. 5.4   B. 5.5   C. 5.6   D. 5.7

3. A capacitor C and inductor L are connected in series across an AC source. As the value of C is increased, the current in the circuit   3.____

    A. increases   B. decreases
    C. remains constant   D. may increase or decrease

4. As the frequency of a generator is decreased, the impedance of a circuit   4.____

    A. increases
    B. decreases
    C. may increase or decrease
    D. does not change

5. It is desired to determine the direction of electron flow in a vertical conductor carrying direct current.   5.____
    This may be done with the aid of a compass placed

    A. to the right of the wire
    B. to the left of the wire
    C. behind the wire
    D. in any of the above listed positions

6. If the current flow in a circular coil consisting of a single turn of wire of 1 cm radius is 2 abamperes, it will produce a magnetic field intensity at the center of the coil equal, in oersteds, to   6.____

    A. π B. 2π C. 4π D. 8π

7. Ampere's Law is concerned with   7.____

    A. the force on a wire carrying a current in a magnetic field
    B. electrochemical equivalents
    C. rms values
    D. unit magnetic poles

8. A 60-watt, 120-volt and a 40-watt, 120-volt lamp are joined in series and connected to a 120-volt line.   8.____
    The current flow in the circuit, in amperes, is

    A. more than 0.5   B. between 0.5 and 0.3
    C. 0.2   D. less than 0.2

90

9. The function of the grid in a three element vacuum tube is to   9._____

    A. aid electron flow at reduced cathode temperatures
    B. reduce the loss of heat from the cathode
    C. prevent secondary emission of electrons from the plate
    D. control the electron flow to the plate

10. Three capacitors of 4 mfd, 10 mfd, and 20 mfd are connected in parallel.   10._____
    The equivalent capacitance of this group equals, in mfd,

    A. 2.5   B. 17   C. 34   D. 800

11. Two 60-watt, 120-volt heaters are connected in series on a 120-volt DC line. The power   11._____
    consumption is now X times as great as it would be if they were connected in parallel.
    Assuming no change in resistance, X would be

    A. 1/4   B. 1/2   C. 2   D. 4

12. The current in an alternating current circuit is equal to the voltage divided by the   12._____

    A. impedance   B. capacitance
    C. reluctance   D. inductance

13. The core of a transformer is laminated largely for the purpose of   13._____

    A. reducing eddy currents
    B. aiding in heat dissipation
    C. increasing self-inductance
    D. increasing impedance

14. Kirchhoff's First Law is really a restatement of   14._____

    A. Lenz' Law
    B. Ohm's Law
    C. Faraday's Law of Electrolysis
    D. Law of Conservation of Energy

15. A condenser designed for use across a 220-volt AC line should have a peak inverse volt-   15._____
    age rating of AT LEAST _____ volts.

    A. 110   B. 220   C. 250   D. 325

16. The voltage between the cathode and target of an x-ray tube is V volts.   16._____
    If e is the charge on the electron in e.s.u., then Ve has the dimensions of

    A. work   B. current   C. force   D. momentum

17. A transformer with 50 turns on the primary and 100 turns on the secondary is connected   17._____
    to a 6-volt battery.
    The voltage on the secondary will be

    A. zero
    B. equal to that on the primary
    C. twice the voltage on the primary
    D. half the voltage on the primary

18. When a 60 cycle source of e.m.f. is connected between the plate and the cathode of a diode, the current between the cathode and plate will

    A. reverse 60 times per second
    B. reverse 120 times per second
    C. flow continuously
    D. flow intermittently in the same direction

18.____

19. Inside a dry cell that is delivering current,

    A. electrons flow from + to -
    B. there is no resistance
    C. there is no current
    D. electrons flow from - to +

19.____

20. In a circuit containing an alternating source and a coil, increasing both the frequency of the source and the inductance of the coil (without changing the e.m.f.) will result in

    A. increased current
    B. decreased current
    C. same current
    D. increased or decreased current, depending on which factor is increased more

20.____

21. If the plate current of a triode electronic tube increases 10 milliamperes when the plate voltage is increased from 60 to 80 volts or when the grid potential changes 2 volts, the amplification factor of the tube is

    A. 5   B. 10   C. 20   D. 40

21.____

22. A series circuit with a capacitive reactance of 20 ohms, an inductive reactance of 50 ohms, and a resistance of 40 ohms has an overall impedance, in ohms, of

    A. 10   B. 50   C. 70   D. 110

22.____

23. Waves of 3 cm in length radiated by an electronic oscillator would have a frequency, in cycles/sec, of

    A. 10^6 B. 10^8 C. 10^{10} D. 10^{12}

23.____

24. If a student, in finding the resistance of a lamp on a 120-volt line, places the voltmeter in series with the lamp and the ammeter in parallel with the lamp, the

    A. ammeter will burn out   B. voltmeter will burn out
    C. lamp will burn out   D. lamp may not light

24.____

25. If a 120-volt, 60-cycle source is connected to a circuit containing resistance, inductive reactance, and capacitive reactance, each of 16 ohms, the current in the circuit is _____ amperes.

    A. 5   B. 7.5   C. 15   D. 30

25.____

26. If a nail is attracted to an electromagnet carrying direct current, and the current is quickly reversed, the nail will   26.____

    A. fall to the ground
    B. be repelled by the electromagnet
    C. heat up
    D. still be attracted

27. The volt is NOT a unit of   27.____

    A. charge per unit time
    C. work per unit charge
    B. e.m.f.
    D. potential difference

28. The energy used to carry unit charge around an electrical circuit is measured by the   28.____

    A. current
    C. power
    B. potential difference
    D. resistance of the circuit

29. Two 1 mfd capacitors are connected in parallel and the combination is then charged. If the capacitance, charge, and potential of each capacitor are C, Q, and V, respectively, the corresponding three values for the combination is which one of the following?   29.____

    A. C/2, 2Q, V
    C. 2C, Q, V
    B. 2C, 2Q, V
    D. 2C, 2Q, V/2

30. The resonant frequency f of an alternating e.m.f. in a circuit containing in series an inductance L, a capacitance C, and a resistance R, is given by the formula f =   30.____

    A. $2\pi\sqrt{LC}$
    B. $\frac{1}{2}\pi\sqrt{LC}$
    C. $\frac{1}{2\pi\sqrt{LC}}$
    D. $\frac{R}{2\pi\sqrt{LC}}$

31. In a series resonant circuit, the circuit impedance is ALWAYS   31.____

    A. equal to the inductive reactance
    B. greater than the capacitive reactance
    C. equal to the capacitive reactance
    D. equal to the resistance

32. Two resistances of 30 ohms and 20 ohms, respectively, are joined in parallel in an electric circuit.
The equivalent resistance, in ohms, of this parallel pair is   32.____

    A. 12
    B. 25
    C. 50
    D. 600

33. A solenoid has an inductance of 0.32 henry.
Its reactance, in ohms, to an alternating current having a frequency of 1000 cycles/sec is   33.____

    A. 2010
    B. 3125
    C. 3200
    D. 3310

34. If, with an impressed voltage of 240 volts and a current of 13 amp, a shunt-wound DC motor delivers 4 horsepower, its efficiency, in percent, is   34.____

    A. 80
    B. 86
    C. 90
    D. 96

35. If the maximum value of an alternating voltage is 110, its value, in volts, at the 30° phase is   35.____

    A. 55   B. 78   C. 155   D. 220

36. A coil of 2.5 henries inductance would resonate with a 1 microfarad capacitance at a frequency, in cycles/sec, of   36.____

    A. 100   B. 1,000   C. 10,000   D. 100,000

37. When an alternating emf is supplied to a circuit consisting, in addition to the source, of wiring a 40 watt lamp and an 80 mf capacitor, the voltage in the circuit   37.____

    A. leads to current
    B. lags behind the current
    C. is in phase with the current
    D. becomes and remains zero after a few minutes

38. Of the following, the one which is incorporated in a DC generator but NOT in an AC generator is the   38.____

    A. slip rings   B. commutator
    C. series field   D. permanent magnets

39. When a capacitor C, an inductance L, and a resistance R are joined in series and an alternating emf is supplied to the circuit, the resonant frequency of this circuit can be decreased by doing which one of the following?   39.____

    A. Increasing L   B. Decreasing R
    C. Decreasing C   D. Decreasing L

40. Three 6 mfd capacitors are connected in parallel across a 120-volt AC line. The equivalent capacitance, in mfd, of this circuit is   40.____

    A. 2   B. 6   C. 18   D. 20

41. Assume that two capacitors, one of 3 microfarad capacitance and the other of 6 microfarad capacitance, are connected in series and charged to a difference of potential of 120 volts.
The potential difference, in volts, across the 3 microfarad capacitor is   41.____

    A. 40   B. 80   C. 180   D. 360

42. Three resistors are connected to form the sides of a triangle ABC. The resistance of side AB is 40 ohms, of side BC 60 ohms, and of side CA 100 ohms.
The effective resistance between points A and B, in ohms, is   42.____

    A. 32   B. 50   C. 64   D. 200

43. When a current of 2 amperes flows through a conductor of 2 ohms resistance for 3 seconds, the heat produced, in joules, is   43.____

    A. 12   B. 24   C. 36   D. 72

44. A length of wire, diameter 2 mils, has a resistance of 6 ohms.
The same length of wire of the same material having a diameter of 4 mils has a resistance, in ohms, of

    A. 1.5   B. 3   C. 12   D. 24

44.____

45. The generalization that the algebraic sum of the currents at a junction in a circuit equals zero was postulated by

    A. Ohm   B. Kirchhoff   C. Onnes   D. Seebeck

45.____

46. It is desired to charge an electroscope negatively by induction.
One of the steps that must be performed is to

    A. use a negatively charged rod
    B. remove positive charges
    C. remove electrons
    D. ground the electroscope

46.____

47. A series AC circuit contains an inductance L, a capacitance C, and a resistor R.
The impedance of this circuit equals

    A. $R^2 + X_L + X_C$ B. $\sqrt{R^2 + (X_L - X_C)^2}$

    C. $R^2 + \sqrt{X_L - X_C}$ D. $R^2 - X_L - X^2_C$

47.____

48. In a selenium rectifier, current flow practically ceases when the

    A. selenium becomes negative
    B. selenium becomes positive
    C. accompanying alloy becomes negative
    D. applied voltage exceeds the critical value

48.____

49. An alternating current generator having 4 poles rotates at 60 revolutions per second.
The frequency of the current produced, in cycles per second, is

    A. 60   B. 15   C. 120   D. 240

49.____

50. If an AC circuit contains resistance only, then current

    A. and voltage are in phase
    B. lags by 45°
    C. leads by 90°
    D. lags by 45° and voltage leads by 45°

50.____

KEY (CORRECT ANSWERS)

1. D	11. A	21. B	31. D	41. B
2. D	12. A	22. B	32. A	42. A
3. D	13. A	23. C	33. A	43. B
4. C	14. D	24. D	34. D	44. A
5. D	15. D	25. B	35. A	45. B
6. C	16. A	26. D	36. A	46. D
7. A	17. A	27. A	37. B	47. B
8. C	18. D	28. B	38. B	48. A
9. D	19. A	29. B	39. A	49. C
10. C	20. B	30. C	40. C	50. A

EXAMINATION SECTION
TEST 1

DIRECTIONS: Each question or incomplete statement is followed by several suggested answers or completions. Select the one that BEST answers the question or completes the statement. *PRINT THE LETTER OF THE CORRECT ANSWER IN THE SPACE AT THE RIGHT.*

1. A piece of equipment listed as drawing 100 watts is plugged into a 24 volt DC circuit. The MINIMUM size fuse which would handle this load is _____ amps.

   A. 2   B. 3   C. 4   D. 5

1._____

2. A resistor of 1000 ohms has 3 milliamperes passing through it. The voltage drop across the resistor is _____ volts.

   A. 3   B. 6   C. 15   D. 300

2._____

3. A certain resistor has three colored bands around it. The one nearest the end is green, the next one is orange, and the next one is red.
The value of this register is _____ ohms.

   A. 74   B. 270   C. 5300   D. 64,000

3._____

4. An alternating voltage is applied to a capacitor.
As the frequency of this voltage is increased, the impedance of the capacitor

   A. increases
   B. decreases
   C. remains the same
   D. increases or decreases depending on its construction

4._____

5. The one of the following that is NOT a part of a transistor is the

   A. emitter   B. collector   C. base   D. grid

5._____

6. A 0.2 ufd capacitor is connected in series with a 0.1 ufd capacitor. The resultant capacity is _____ ufd.

   A. 0.067   B. 0.67   C. 0.15   D. 0.3

6._____

7. The term *Hertz* means the same as

   A. degrees Centigrade   B. degrees Fahrenheit
   C. revolutions per minute   D. cycles per second

7._____

8. In an electrolytic condenser, the dielectric material is

   A. mylar   B. aluminum oxide
   C. paper   D. sodium chloride

8._____

9. The amount by which a transformer will step up or step down a voltage is determined by its

   A. inductance   B. resistance
   C. magnetic flux   D. turns ratio

9._____

10. The electrolyte in a lead plate storage battery (such as that used in cars) is   10._____

    A. aluminum hydroxide   B. sulfuric acid
    C. hydrochloric acid   D. sodium chloride

11. A diode in an electronic circuit is used to   11._____

    A. amplify   B. oscillate   C. attenuate   D. rectify

12. The MAIN function of a filter in a power supply is to   12._____

    A. increase the voltage
    B. decrease the load
    C. smooth out the peaks of the ripple frequency
    D. protect the power transformer

13. The expression *pH* as applied to a liquid refers to its   13._____

    A. salinity   B. specific gravity
    C. viscosity   D. acidity/alkalinity

14. The speed of a synchronous motor is controlled by   14._____

    A. the voltage applied to it
    B. the frequency of the alternating current applied to it
    C. a mechanical governor
    D. the current it draws

15. The capacitance of a condenser is measured in   15._____

    A. oersteds   B. ohms   C. henrys   D. farads

16. The power lost in a 20-ohm resistor, with 0.25 amperes passing through it, is _____ watts.   16._____

    A. 0.04   B. 0.4   C. 1.25   D. 5

17. When soldering a transistor into a circuit, it is good practice to clamp a pair of long-nosed pliers on the lead between the transistor and the end being soldered.
This is done to   17._____

    A. prevent the lead from moving
    B. prevent burning the fingers
    C. ground the transistor
    D. prevent the soldering iron's heat from reaching the transistor

18. The commutator of a motor should   18._____

    A. not be lubricated
    B. be lubricated with light oil
    C. be lubricated with heavy grease
    D. be lubricated with hypoid oil

19. The band of wavelengths of visible light covers   19._____

    A. 20-50 centimeters   B. 10-50 meters
    C. 400-700 millimicrons   D. 400-700 millimeters

20. The heat reaching the earth from the sun is transmitted by   20.____

    A. ions   B. convection
    C. radiation   D. cosmic rays

21. A *thermistor* is a   21.____

    A. type of thermometer
    B. high power transistor
    C. water heating device
    D. resistor with a negative temperature coefficient

22. In an AC circuit, the term *power factor* refers to the   22.____

    A. horsepower
    B. BTU per watt
    C. ratio of the resistance to the impedance
    D. kilowatts per horsepower

23.   23.____

In the above circuit, the TOTAL resistance between points A and B is _____ ohms.

    A. 5   B. 14   C. 20   D. 45

24. Of the four gases listed below, the one that is NOT an air pollutant is   24.____

    A. carbon dioxide   B. carbon monoxide
    C. sulfur dioxide   D. hydrogen sulfide

25. The term *milli-roentgen* refers to a unit of   25.____

    A. x-ray radiation   B. ultraviolet radiation
    C. reluctance   D. inductance

26. An AC motor drawing 12 amps is plugged into a 15-amp circuit. The starting surge of the   26.____
motor, however, is 18 amps.
The PROPER type of fuse to be used in this situation is

    A. varistor   B. thermistor
    C. fast-blow   D. slow-blow

27. Degrees Kelvin is numerically equal to degrees   27.____

    A. Fahrenheit - 15   B. Centigrade + 27
    C. Fahrenheit + 135   D. Centigrade + 273

28. In the term *micromicrofarads*, the prefix *micromicro* means multiply by   28.____

    A. 10^6 B. 10^3 C. 10^{-12} D. 10^{-6}

29. One horsepower is equivalent to   29.____

    A. 276 joules   B. 746 kilowatts
    C. 746 watts   D. 291 calories

30. Laminated iron or steel is generally used instead of solid metal in the construction of the   30.____
field and armature cores in motors and generators.
The reason for this is to

    A. reduce eddy current losses
    B. increase the voltage
    C. decrease the flux
    D. reduce the cost

31. The instrument used to measure current flow is called a(n)   31.____

    A. wattmeter   B. voltmeter
    C. ammeter   D. wavemeter

32. Reversing the polarity of the voltage applied to a mica condenser will   32.____

    A. destroy it   B. increase its capacity
    C. decrease its capacity   D. have no effect on it

33. The *decibel* is the unit used for expressing   33.____

    A. light levels
    B. DC voltage
    C. AC current
    D. the ratio between two quantities of either electrical or sound energy

34. In a three-phase Y-connected AC power system, the voltage from leg to ground is 120   34.____
volts.
The voltage between each pair of hot legs is _____ volts.

    A. 160   B. 180   C. 208   D. 240

35. An hygrometer is an instrument which measures   35.____

    A. humidity   B. temperature
    C. specific gravity   D. luminosity

36. The impedance ratio of a transformer varies _____ the turns ratio.   36.____

    A. directly with   B. as the square of
    C. as the square root of   D. inversely with

37. Two resistors are connected in series. The current through these resistors is 3 amperes.   37.____
Resistance #1 has a value of fifty ohms; resistance #2 has a voltage drop of fifty volts
across its terminals.
The TOTAL impressed voltage (across both resistors) is _____ volts.

    A. 100   B. 150   C. 200   D. 250

38. The piece of equipment that should be used to obtain more than one voltage from a fixed voltage direct current source is a(n) 38.____

   A. multitap transformer
   B. resistance-type voltage divider
   C. autotransformer
   D. copper oxide rectifier

39. The ratio of peak to effective (rms) voltage value of a sine wave is 39.____

   A. 2 to 1 B. 1 to 2 C. .707 to 1 D. 1.414 to 1

40. Two coils are connected in series.
If there is no mutual inductance between the coils, the TOTAL inductance of the two coils is the _____ inductances. 40.____

   A. sum of the individual
   B. product of the individual
   C. product of the square roots of the two
   D. sum of the squares of the individual

41. The impedance of a coil with zero resistance is called the 41.____

   A. reluctance B. conductance
   C. inductive reactance D. flux

42. The ratio of the energy stored to the energy lost in a coil over a period of one cycle is called its 42.____

   A. efficiency B. Q
   C. reactance D. resistance

43. In a vacuum tube, the current is carried by 43.____

   A. ions B. neutrons C. electrons D. molecules

44. The device used to vary the intensity of an incandescent light on a 120V AC circuit is a 44.____

   A. variable capacitor
   B. silicon controlled rectifier
   C. copper oxide rectifier
   D. rf amplifier

45. High power transistors must be mounted on *heat sinks.* The purpose of the heat sinks is to 45.____

   A. improve voltage regulation
   B. increase the transistors' output
   C. keep the transistors warm
   D. keep the transistors cool

46. The one of the following materials that has the HIGHEST conductivity is 46.____

   A. iron B. zinc C. copper D. silver

47. The unit used to express the alternating current impedance of a circuit is the   47.____

    A. mho   B. farad   C. ohm   D. rel

48. A certain resistor has four colored bands on it. The fourth band is gold.   48.____
This means that the resistor

    A. is wirewound   B. is non-inductive
    C. has a ± 20% tolerance   D. has a ± 5% tolerance

49. An amplifier has an output voltage waveform that does not exactly follow that of the input   49.____
voltage.
This type of distortion is called _____ distortion.

    A. modular   B. frequency
    C. resonance   D. amplitude

50. A parallel circuit, resonant at 1000 khz, has its value of capacity doubled and its value of   50.____
inductance halved.
Its resonant frequency now is _____ khz.

    A. 500   B. 1000   C. 1500   D. 2000

KEY (CORRECT ANSWERS)

1. D	11. D	21. D	31. C	41. C
2. A	12. C	22. C	32. D	42. B
3. C	13. D	23. B	33. D	43. C
4. B	14. B	24. A	34. C	44. B
5. D	15. D	25. A	35. A	45. D
6. A	16. C	26. D	36. B	46. D
7. D	17. D	27. D	37. C	47. C
8. B	18. A	28. C	38. B	48. D
9. D	19. C	29. C	39. D	49. D
10. B	20. C	30. A	40. A	50. B

TEST 2

DIRECTIONS: Each question or incomplete statement is followed by several suggested answers or completions. Select the one that BEST answers the question or completes the statement. *PRINT THE LETTER OF THE CORRECT ANSWER IN THE SPACE AT THE RIGHT.*

1. A voltmeter which reads 100V full scale has a specified accuracy of 3%. It is hooked across a circuit and reads 97 volts.
   The TRUE voltage can be assumed to be somewhere between

   A. 96.7 and 97.3
   C. 96.07 and 97.03
   B. 94 and 100
   D. 95.5 and 98.5

   1.____

2. The product of 127.2 and .0037 is

   A. 4706.4   B. 470.64   C. .47064   D. .0047064

   2.____

3. The wind velocity at a certain location was measured four times in a 24-hour period. The readings were 32 mph, 10 mph, 16 mph, and 2 mph.
   The AVERAGE wind velocity for that day was _____ mph.

   A. 24   B. 20   C. 15   D. 13

   3.____

4. When 280 is divided by .014, the answer is

   A. .002   B. 20   C. 200   D. 20,000

   4.____

5. The square root of 289 is

   A. 1.7   B. 9.7   C. 17   D. 144.5

   5.____

6. The watts drawn by a resistive load is to be determined. To do this, a voltmeter (10V full scale) is connected across the load, and an ammeter (10 amps full scale) is connected in series with the load. Both instruments are specified as having 1% (full scale) accuracy. The voltmeter reads 9.2V; the ammeter reads 8.3 amps.
   The MOST valid value for the watts drawn is _____ watts.

   A. 76   B. 76.36   C. 76.4   D. 80

   6.____

7. The formula for converting degrees Centigrade to degrees Fahrenheit is: $^\circ F = (9/5).(^\circ C) + 32$.
   A temperature of 25° C is equal to

   A. 102.6° F   B. 85° F   C. 77° F   D. 43° F

   7.____

8. The prefix *kilo* means

   A. multiply by one million
   B. divide by one million
   C. multiply by one thousand
   D. divide by one hundred

   8.____

9. 2^8 is equal to

   A. 512   B. 256   C. 124   D. 82

   9.____

10. The prefix *milli* means   10.____

    A. multiply by 100   B. divide by one thousand
    C. divide by one million   D. multiply by one million

11. If $1/X = 1/20 + 1/20 + 1/40$, the value of X is   11.____

    A. .125   B. 8   C. 16   D. 20

12. 2×10^6 multiplied by 4×10^{-6} equals   12.____

    A. 8   B. 8×10^{-12} C. 8×10^{12} D. 8×10^3

13. 1 inch equals _____ cm.   13.____

    A. 0.62   B. 2.54   C. 3.94   D. 16.2

14. 1 kg equals   14.____

    A. 2.2 lbs.   B. 17.3 oz.   C. 0.52 lbs.   D. 12 oz.

15. 1 liter equals   15.____

    A. 3.78 quarts   B. 1.057 quarts
    C. 1.39 pints   D. .067 gallons

16. A circle has a radius of 10 inches.   16.____
    Its circumference is _____ inches.

    A. 72.3   B. 62.8   C. 31.4   D. 25

17. A right angle triangle has sides measuring 3 inches and 4 inches; its hypotenuse is 5   17.____
    inches.
    The area of this triangle is _____ square inches.

    A. 6   B. 20   C. 15   D. 60

18. A square has an area of 81 square inches.   18.____
    The length of each side is _____ inches.

    A. 7.9   B. 9   C. 11   D. 17

19. A bottle contains 11 pints of liquid. To this bottle 1.32 pints is then added.   19.____
    This is an increase of

    A. 6%   B. 9%   C. 12%   D. 16%

20. A week ago a storage battery read 12.4V. Today its voltage is 8.1% less.   20.____
    Its voltage is now

    A. 11.4   B. 10.8   C. 9.3   D. 10.2

21. The advantage of a vacuum tube voltmeter over a regular voltmeter is that it   21.____

    A. operates on batteries
    B. operates on 120V AC
    C. has a low input impedance
    D. has a high input impedance

22. A g_m tube tester measures a vacuum tube's   22.____

    A. capacitance   B. resistance
    C. emission   D. transconductance

23. A cathode ray tube is used in a(n)   23.____

    A. audio amplifier   B. radio frequency amplifier
    C. oscilloscope   D. volt-ohm-milliammeter

24. A voltmeter is described as having *1000 ohms per volt*. The current required to produce   24.____
full scale deflection is

    A. 1 milliampere   B. 1 ampere
    C. 20 milliamperes   D. 0.05 milliamperes

25. The PRIMARY use of a test oscilloscope is to   25.____

    A. analyze complex waveforms
    B. measure resistance
    C. measure capacitance
    D. measure DC voltages

26. A spectrophotometer is an instrument that measures   26.____

    A. photographic film density
    B. the amount of light of a particular wavelength
    C. the amount of airborne dust
    D. x-ray radiation

27. The test instrument generally known as a *multitester* will measure, among other things,   27.____

    A. temperature   B. beta radiation
    C. AC watts   D. DC milliamperes

28. A lightmeter used in measuring incident light gives readings in   28.____

    A. footcandles   B. candlepower
    C. lumens   D. foot-lamberts

29. A selenium photocell is a type known as photo-   29.____

    A. emissive   B. resistive
    C. voltaic   D. transistive

30. In wiring electronic circuits, the solder GENERALLY used is _____ solder.   30.____

    A. silver   B. acid core
    C. aluminum   D. rosin core

31. An unconscious victim of electric shock should be orally administered   31.____

    A. nothing
    B. coffee
    C. alcohol
    D. aromatic apirits of ammonia

32. Persons operating x-ray equipment should wear   32.____

    A. safety goggles
    B. insulating gloves
    C. a lead-coated apron and gloves
    D. a surgical mask

33. Harmful radiation is emitted by the element   33.____

    A. neon   B. lithium   C. platinum   D. radium

34. When a victim of electrical shock or near drowning is given artificial respiration and he does not appear to respond, the treatment should continue for at least   34.____

    A. four hours   B. fifteen minutes
    C. five minutes   D. fifteen hours

35. A person maintaining high voltage equipment should avoid wearing   35.____

    A. long hair
    B. sneakers
    C. rings and metallic watchbands
    D. eyeglasses

36. Portable AC equipment is often equipped with a three-wire cable and a three-prong male plug.
The reason for this is to prevent   36.____

    A. radiation   B. electric shock
    C. oscillation   D. ground currents

37. Smoke is seen issuing from a piece of electronic equipment. The FIRST thing that should be done is to   37.____

    A. call the fire department
    B. pour water on it
    C. look for a fire extinguisher
    D. shut off the power

38. A match should not be used when inspecting the electrolyte level in a lead-acid battery because the cells emit   38.____

    A. nitrogen   B. hydrogen
    C. carbon dioxide   D. sulfur dioxide

39. A person feels nauseated, his mental capacity has been lowered, and he has a severe throbbing headache. It is suspected that he has been poisoned by gas, but there is no apparent odor.
The poisonous gas is MOST likely to be   39.____

    A. sulfur dioxide   B. hydrogen cyanide
    C. carbon monoxide   D. chlorine

40. The purpose of an interlock on a piece of electronic equipment is to

    A. prevent theft of the vacuum tubes
    B. prevent electrical shock to maintenance personnel
    C. prevent rf radiation
    D. keep the equipment cool

40.____

41. An alternating voltage is applied to an inductance.
    As the frequency of the voltage is decreased, the impedance of the inductance

    A. decreases
    B. increases
    C. follows the alternating voltage
    D. remains the same

41.____

42. A 0.25 ufd condenser is connected in parallel with a 0.50 ufd condenser.
    The resultant capacity is _____ ufd.

    A. 0.167   B. 0.37   C. 0.75   D. 2.5

42.____

43. The electrolyte in a carbon-zinc dry cell is

    A. sulfuric acid   B. ammonium chloride
    C. lithium chloride   D. sodium chloride

43.____

44. A 5000-ohm resistor has a voltage of 25 volts applied to it.
    The current drawn by the resistor is

    A. 5 milliamperes   B. 5 amperes
    C. 75 milliamperes   D. 1.25 milliamperes

44.____

45. A certain resistor has three colored bands around it.
    The one nearest the end is red, the next one is gray, and the next one is yellow.
    The value of the resistor is

    A. 2.7 megaohms   B. 280,000 ohms
    C. 3270 ohms   D. 449 ohms

45.____

Questions 46-50.

DIRECTIONS: Questions 46 through 50 are to be answered on the basis of the following
              paragraph.

    The second half of the twin triode acts as a phase modulator. The rf output of the crystal oscillator is impressed on the phase-modulator grid by means of a blocking condenser. The cathode circuit is provided with a large amount of degeneration by an un-bypassed cathode resistor. Because of this degenerative feedback, the transconductance of the triode is abnormally low, so low that the plate current is affected as much by the direct grid-plate capacitance as by the transconductance. The two effects result in plate current vectors almost 180° apart, and the total plate current is the resultant of the two components. In phase, it will be about 90° removed from the phase of the voltage impressed on the grid.

46. As used in the above paragraph, the word *impressed* means MOST NEARLY
    A. applied   B. blocked   C. changed   D. detached

    46._____

47. As used in the above paragraph, the word *components* refers to the
    A. blocking condenser and cathode resistor
    B. twin triode
    C. plate current vectors
    D. grid-plate capacitance

    47._____

48. According to the above paragraph, degenerative feedback is obtained by means of
    A. a crystal oscillator
    B. the plate voltage
    C. an un-bypassed cathode resistor
    D. a blocking condenser

    48._____

49. According to the above paragraph, the cathode resistor is
    A. very large
    B. not bypassed
    C. in series with an inductance
    D. shunted by a blocking condenser

    49._____

50. According to the above paragraph, the phase angle between the grid voltage and the total plate current is APPROXIMATELY
    A. 180°   B. 90°   C. 270°   D. zero

    50._____

KEY (CORRECT ANSWERS)

1.	B	11.	B	21.	D	31.	A	41.	A
2.	C	12.	C	22.	D	32.	C	42.	C
3.	C	13.	B	23.	C	33.	D	43.	B
4.	D	14.	A	24.	A	34.	A	44.	A
5.	C	15.	B	25.	A	35.	C	45.	B
6.	A	16.	B	26.	B	36.	B	46.	A
7.	C	17.	A	27.	D	37.	D	47.	C
8.	C	18.	B	28.	A	38.	B	48.	C
9.	B	19.	C	29.	C	39.	C	49.	B
10.	B	20.	A	30.	D	40.	B	50.	B

EXAMINATION SECTION
TEST 1

DIRECTIONS: Each question or incomplete statement is followed by several suggested answers or completions. Select the one that BEST answers the question or completes the statement. *PRINT THE LETTER OF THE CORRECT ANSWER IN THE SPACE AT THE RIGHT.*

1. Suppose a man falls from a two-story high scaffold and is unconscious. You should   1.____

    A. call for medical assistance and avoid moving the man
    B. get someone to help you move him indoors to a bed
    C. have someone help you walk him around until he revives
    D. hold his head up and pour a stimulant down his throat

2. For proper first aid treatment, a person who has fainted should be   2.____

    A. doused with cold water and then warmly covered
    B. given artificial respiration until he is revived
    C. laid down with his head lower than the rest of his body
    D. slapped on the face until he is revived

3. If you are called on to give first aid to a person who is suffering from shock, you should   3.____

    A. apply cold towels   B. give him a stimulant
    C. keep him awake   D. wrap him warmly

4. Artificial respiration would NOT be a proper first aid for a person suffering from   4.____

    A. drowning   B. electric shock
    C. external bleeding   D. suffocation

5. Suppose you are called on to give first aid to several victims of an accident. FIRST attention should be given to the one who is   5.____

    A. bleeding severely   B. groaning loudly
    C. unconscious   D. vomiting

6. Of the following, the MOST serious defect in first aid actions taken at the scene of accidents is, generally, the failure   6.____

    A. of someone to take command of the situation
    B. to examine the victim thoroughly for injuries
    C. to keep the patient warm and comfortable
    D. to summon an ambulance immediately

7. Concerning first aid actions taken at the scene of an accident, it would be MOST COR-RECT to state that   7.____

    A. a compress should never be used for direct pressure in arterial bleeding
    B. it is at least as important to know what actions should not be taken as to take the proper action
    C. the first aider should not make a decision as to the nature of the victim's injuries
    D. the victim should be informed of the nature and extent of serious injuries

8. An injured person who is unconscious should NOT be given a liquid to drink mainly because

    A. cold liquid may be harmful
    B. he may choke on it
    C. he may not like the liquid
    D. his unconsciousness may be due to too much liquid

8.____

9. The MOST important reason for putting a bandage on a cut is to

    A. help prevent germs from getting into the cut
    B. hide the ugly scar
    C. keep the blood pressure down
    D. keep the skin warm

9.____

10. In first aid for an injured person, the main purpose of a tourniquet is to

    A. prevent infection   B. restore circulation
    C. support a broken bone   D. stop severe bleeding

10.____

11. Artificial respiration is given in first aid mainly to

    A. force air into the lungs
    B. force blood circulation by even pressure
    C. keep the injured person awake
    D. prevent shock by keeping the victim's body in motion

11.____

12. The aromatic spirits of ammonia in a first aid kit should be used to

    A. clean a dirty wound
    B. deaden pain
    C. revive a person who has fainted
    D. warm a person who is chilled

12.____

13. First aid for a person who has fainted is

    A. administer a hot beverage
    B. hold the head back and open the mouth
    C. administer aromatic spirits of ammonia
    D. lower the head below heart level

13.____

14. To reduce swelling, one should apply

    A. hot applications   B. cold applications
    C. a bandage   D. an electric heating pad

14.____

15. First aid for poisoning by mouth: The FIRST step is to

    A. telephone the doctor
    B. save the label on the box of poison
    C. dilute the poison
    D. administer antidote of strong tea, milk of magnesia, and crumbled burned toast

15.____

16. Treat a chemical burn with   16._____

    A. mild iodine and a sterile dressing
    B. quantities of clear water
    C. light bandage
    D. soap dressing

17. For wounds in which bleeding is NOT severe,   17._____

    A. cleanse thoroughly using plain soap and running water
    B. wash the wound with peroxide
    C. clean the area with iodine 3 1/2% in alcohol 70%
    D. bandage after applying lysol

18. The BEST immediate first aid for a scraped knee is to   18._____

    A. apply plain vaseline   B. apply an ice pack
    C. apply heat   D. wash it with soap and water

19. In treating injuries, it is MOST important that any bandages used be   19._____

    A. clean   B. damp
    C. large   D. waterproof

20. Of the following, the BEST first aid treatment for a second degree burn is to cover the burn with a   20._____

    A. thin, wet sterile dressing
    B. thin, dry sterile dressing
    C. thick, wet sterile dressing
    D. thick, dry sterile dressing

21. One of the laborers on the job feels unusually tired, has headache and nausea, is perspiring heavily, and the skin is pale and clammy. He is PROBABLY suffering from   21._____

    A. epilepsy   B. food poisoning
    C. heat exhaustion   D. sunstroke

22. If a laborer feels faint, the BEST advice to give him is   22._____

    A. lie flat with his head low
    B. walk around till he revives
    C. run around till he revives
    D. drink a glass of cold water

23. In first aid, a tourniquet is MOST often used to   23._____

    A. improve respiration   B. treat burns
    C. treat sprains   D. control bleeding

24. Persons who have been injured may suffer a depressed condition of many of the body functions due to failure of enough blood to circulate through the body. This condition is called   24._____

    A. immunization   B. chronic
    C. cathartic   D. shock

25. The type of injury which is MOST likely to cause lockjaw (tetanus) is

    A. an epileptic convulsion   B. a puncture wound
    C. an electric shock   D. sunstroke

25.____

KEY (CORRECT ANSWERS)

1.	A		11.	A
2.	C		12.	C
3.	D		13.	D
4.	C		14.	B
5.	A		15.	C
6.	A		16.	B
7.	D		17.	A
8.	B		18.	D
9.	A		19.	A
10.	D		20.	D

21.	C
22.	A
23.	D
24.	D
25.	B

TEST 2

DIRECTIONS: Each question or incomplete statement is followed by several suggested answers or completions. Select the one that BEST answers the question or completes the statement. *PRINT THE LETTER OF THE CORRECT ANSWER IN THE SPACE AT THE RIGHT.*

1. Of the following topics in first aid, the one which usually involves the MOST extensive study or review of anatomy is:

    A. First degree burns   B. Pressure points
    C. Dog bites   D. Convulsions

1.____

2. According to the American Red Cross, the dislocation that a person trained in first aid should NOT attempt to reduce is a dislocation of the

    A. lower jaw
    B. first joint of the big toe
    C. second joint of the index finger
    D. second joint of the thumb

2.____

3. Internal bleeding which is usually vomited up and has the appearance of coffee grounds is bleeding from the

    A. bowels   B. stomach   C. liver   D. lungs

3.____

4. The symptoms of heat exhaustion are

    A. pale, clammy skin, low temperature, weak pulse
    B. rapid and strong pulse, dry skin, high temperature
    C. headache, red face, unconsciousness
    D. abdominal cramps, red skin, profuse sweating

4.____

5. The "back-pressure, arm-lift" method of artificial respiration is superior to other methods because it

    A. eliminates the use of the inhalator
    B. is comparable to normal respiration in regard to oxygen intake
    C. increases compression of the chest by application of rhythmic pressure of the lower ribs
    D. is similar to the action in which a person inflates his chest by taking deep breaths

5.____

6. Arterial pressure points

    A. are best located by taking the pulse
    B. lie close to bones near the surface of the body
    C. are used to cut off all blood circulation
    D. are deep-seated and require great pressure

6.____

7. Of the following, the one NOT recommended for the first aid care of burns is

    A. boric acid   B. baking soda
    C. petrolatum ointment   D. epsom salts

7.____

8. The FIRST step in the treatment of a person who is injured, unconscious, and bleeding profusely is to

    8.____

    A. call a doctor
    B. stop the bleeding
    C. remove the person to a hospital
    D. revive the person

9. In treating heat exhaustion, it is imperative that you FIRST

    9.____

    A. treat for shock
    B. move the patient to a place where the air is as fresh and cool as possible
    C. keep the body warmly covered
    D. lay the patient with his head low

10. While on duty, an officer sees a woman apparently in a state of shock. Of the following, which one is NOT a symptom of shock?

    10.____

    A. Eyes lacking luster
    B. A cold, moist forehead
    C. A shallow, irregular breathing
    D. A strong, throbbing pulse

11. You notice a man entering your building who begins coughing violently, has shortness of breath, and complains of severe chest pains. These symptoms are GENERALLY indicative of

    11.____

    A. a heart attack   B. a stroke
    C. internal bleeding   D. an epileptic seizure

12. The PROPER immediate first aid care for a frostbitten hand is to

    12.____

    A. rub the hand with snow
    B. place the part in warm water
    C. cover the hand with a woolen cloth
    D. vigorously rub the hands together

13. A person who has fainted should be

    13.____

    A. propped up on a pillow or head rest
    B. given a warm drink
    C. aroused as soon as possible
    D. laid flat and kept quiet

14. Of the following associations of symptom(s) and sudden illness or accident, the INCORRECT one is

    14.____

    A. blood spurting from the wrist-cut artery
    B. stoppage of breathing - suffocation
    C. pale, cold, moist skin - shock
    D. partial tearing of ligaments of a joint - strain

15. In the care of a sprained ankle, an INCORRECT procedure in first aid would be to   15.____

    A. elevate the sprained part
    B. apply cold applications
    C. massage the part to restore circulation
    D. apply a temporary support

16. In administering first aid, one should encourage bleeding by mild pressure, being careful   16.____
not to bruise the tissue, in wounds classified as

    A. punctures   B. incisions
    C. lacerations   D. abrasions

17. All of the following first aid rules for simple nosebleed may be safely followed EXCEPT   17.____

    A. gently pinching the nostrils together
    B. applying cold compresses to the nose
    C. blowing the nose gently after bleeding stops to remove blood clots
    D. inserting a plug of absorbent cotton in each of the nostrils

Questions 18-20.

Questions 18 to 20 are based on the situation described below.

While conducting a special investigation of a power distribution fault, a maintainer working with you alone accidentally receives a severe, electric shock and falls on his back
unconscious, with one hand badly burned. He is not in contact with the live circuit. There
are no traffic hazards.

18. The FIRST thing you should do is to   18.____

    A. determine if the victim is breathing
    B. go to nearest telephone and call your supervisor
    C. turn the victim over on his stomach
    D. cover the burned hand to protect it from air

19. You start artificial resuscitation and shortly afterward another employee arrives at the   19.____
scene of the accident and prepares to relieve you. In this case,

    A. the change should be made at the count of "three" while hands are on the victim
       applying pressure
    B. you should skip one cycle to make the changeover
    C. both operators should apply pressure together for two cycles before second opera-
       tor proceeds alone
    D. the change should be made at the count of "one" while hands are off the victim's
       body

20. When the victim starts breathing naturally but is still unconscious,   20.____

    A. he must be watched carefully in case breathing stops
    B. he should be given a stimulating drink immediately
    C. resuscitation must be continued for 15 minutes longer
    D. clothing around the victim's throat and chest should be removed

21. Statistics compiled by the safety bureau of the transit system indicate that less than one employee in ten is a qualified first aider, and that nearly one out of every five employees met with an accident during the past year. The ONLY correct statement that can be made from these figures is that

    A. one-half of the accidents occurred without a qualified first aider present
    B. the number of accidents was about twice the number of qualified first aiders
    C. there would be fewer accidents if there were more trained first aiders
    D. all transit employees should be qualified first aiders

21._____

22. First aid kits are sealed, and any person who opens the kit must make a report setting forth the reason for opening the kit. together with the kind and amount of material used. The MAIN purpose for requiring this report is to

    A. replenish the necessary supplies
    B. determine who used the kit last
    C. decide if the user had proper knowledge of first aid
    D. discourage the use of these kits

22._____

23. In treating a victim of nosebleed, of the following the LEAST effective procedure is to

    A. have the victim lie down immediately
    B. press the nostrils firmly together
    C. apply a large, cold, wet cloth to the nose
    D. pack the nose gently with gauze

23._____

24. In first aid, the overall purpose of the application of heat to a victim in shock is to

    A. produce sweating
    B. prevent a large loss of body heat
    C. increase the temperature of the body
    D. increase the circulation of the blood

24._____

25. Of the following, the PRIME responsibility of the first aider is to

    A. apply a splint to a fracture
    B. treat for shock
    C. help the patient to regain consciousness
    D. reduce a dislocation

25.____

KEY (CORRECT ANSWERS)

1.	B		11.	A
2.	D		12.	C
3.	B		13.	D
4.	A		14.	D
5.	D		15.	C
6.	B		16.	A
7.	A		17.	C
8.	B		18.	A
9.	B		19.	D
10.	D		20.	A

21.	D
22.	A
23.	A
24.	B
25.	B

―――――――

ELECTRO-MECHANICAL
NOTES AND RESOURCES

TABLE OF CONTENTS

ELECTRO-MECHANICAL
NOTES AND RESOURCES
I. BASIC ELECTRICITY

Resistance is measured in ohms, and its symbol is Ω. Resistance is additive in series circuits. This means that with two resistors in series as shown below, if one resistor is 100Ω's and the other 200Ω's, then the total resistance is 300Ω's.

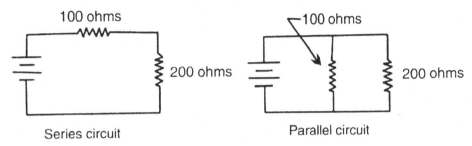

Series circuit   Parallel circuit

Resistance in parallel is summed differently. In the figure shown above in the parallel circuit, if the 100 ohm resistor is considered to be R, and the 200 ohm resistor is R, the formula is:

$$\frac{1}{R_t} = \frac{1}{R_1} + \frac{1}{R_2}.$$

Derivation is as follows:

$$\frac{1}{R_1} = (\frac{1}{R_1} \times \frac{R_2}{R_2}) + (\frac{1}{R_2} \times \frac{R_1}{R_1}) = \frac{R_1}{R_1 R_2} + \frac{R_1}{R_1 R_2} = \frac{R_1 + R_2}{R_1 R_2}$$

So, now we have:

$$\frac{1}{R_t} = \frac{R_1 + R_2}{R_1 R_2}. \text{ Inversing, } \frac{R_t}{1} = \frac{R_1 R_2}{R_1 + R_2} = R_t$$

This derivation is for two resistors in parallel; for more resistors in parallel, the same derivation technique would be followed.

Given that all the resistors in a parallel circuit are of the same resistive value, the following is a short calculation of the total circuit resistance.

Take the resistive value of one of the resistors and divide it by the number of resistors in the parallel circuit. Assuming that 5 resistors are in parallel and each one is 500 ohms, to calculate the total circuit resistance, divide 500 by 5 and the result is 100 ohms.

An interesting aspect of resistance is that the inverse (1/R) is conduction, the ease with which electrons can flow through a given material, and is expressed in units of *mhos* with a symbol that is the same as the resistance symbol inverted.

The color codes for resistors are as follows:

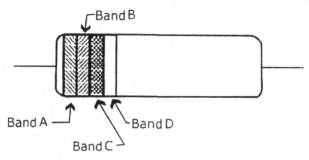

Band A is the first digit of the value of the resistor.
Band B is the second digit of the value of the resistor.
Band C is the decimal multiplier.
Band D is the tolerance of the value of the resistor.

The colors and their values are:

COLOR	VALUE	COLOR	VALUE	TOLERANCE COLORS
BLACK	0	GREEN	5	
BROWN	1	BLUE	6	GOLD 5%
RED	2	VIOLET	7	SILVER 10%
ORANGE	3	GRAY	8	NO COLOR 20%
YELLOW	4	WHITE	9	

So, a resistor colored as:

1st band	violet
2nd band	green
3rd band	blue
4th band	silver

is computed as:

An easy way of remembering the sequence of the color codes above is to remember the following sentence and use the first letters of each word: *Bad Boys Race Our Young Girls Behind Victory Garden Walls*.

Ohms' Law

Ohm's law is the law that establishes the mathematical relationship of current, voltage, and resistance in a circuit. The formula is: $E = IR$, where E = the circuit or component voltage, I = the circuit or component current, and R = the circuit or component resistance.

In the circuit shown below, we know $E = 10$ volts and $I = 5$ ohms. Deriving the formula, we get $I = E/R$. So, $I = 10/5 = 2$ amps.

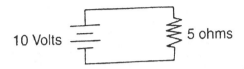

10 Volts — 5 ohms

The power consumed by a component is equal to E x I. So, P = EI, and this calculated value is expressed in units of watts.

Kirchoff's Voltage Law

Kirchoff's voltage law states in technical terms that in a simple series circuit, as shown below, the algebraic sum of the voltages around the circuit is zero. Basically, this means that the supply voltage, Vsupply, is equal to VA + VB + VC, which are the voltage drops across the respective resistors in the circuit below. In the parallel circuit shown below, the voltages in each of the individual branches are equal to each other as well as equal to the total circuit voltage.

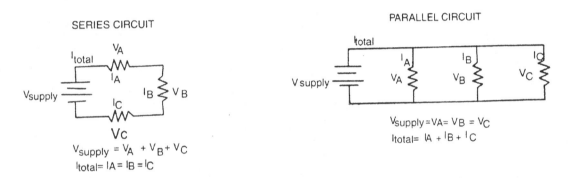

SERIES CIRCUIT

$V_{supply} = V_A + V_B + V_C$
$I_{total} = I_A = I_B = I_C$

PARALLEL CIRCUIT

$V_{supply} = V_A = V_B = V_C$
$I_{total} = I_A + I_B + I_C$

Kirchoff's Current Law

Kirchoff's current law states that at any junction of conductors in a circuit, the algebraic sum of the currents is zero. On a series circuit shown above, current is equal across each individual component as well as equal to the total circuit current. In a parallel circuit, the current across each individual branch when added is equal to the total circuit current, as in the parallel circuit shown above.

Inductors

Inductors are coils that oppose changes in current, which also store energy in a magnetic field. Induction is expressed in units of henries, and represented by an h. Inductance in series and parallel circuits is summed in the same manner as resistance. Inductors tend to block AC signals and pass DC voltages. An inductor's ability to oppose AC current is called inductive reactance. Inductive reactance is expressed in ohms just like resistance, but is represented by the symbol ZL, where Z means impedance and L added specifies inductive reactance or impedance. The impedance symbol Ω should not be confused with the resistive symbol, which is the same. The formula for inductive reactance is: $XL = 2 \pi fL$, where $\pi = 3.14$, f = the frequency of the AC signal to be used, and L = the inductance in henries. The schematic symbol for an inductor is ⌇⌇⌇

Adding two lines on the top of the symbol means that it is an iron core filled inductor. Since they have a magnetic field, they are used in transformers and electromagnetic switches.

Capacitors

Capacitors consist basically of two metal plates in parallel separated by an insulator (dielectric). Capacitors have the ability to store a charge in an electrostatic field between its two plates. This charge is dependent upon two things, the capacitance of the circuit and the difference in the potential of the circuit. The capacitance of a capacitor is measured in farads, and is depicted by the letter C. Capacitance is summed in a manner that is exactly opposite to that of resistors, since it is directly summed when in parallel as shown below.

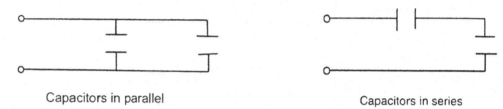

Capacitors in parallel   Capacitors in series

In the parallel circuit shown above, if one of the capacitors is 1 farad and the other is 2 farads, then total circuit capacitance is 3 farads. Capacitance of such a high value is rare and usually limited to industrial use. More realistic values would be in the microfarad range. When capacitors are in series as shown above, they are added, as are resistors in

parallel. So, the formula would be: $Ct = \dfrac{C_1 C_2}{C_1 + C_2}$

As with inductors, capacitors are also measured by the opposition that they may give to AC current flow, which is called capacitive reactance. Capacitive reactance, X_c, is expressed also in units of ohms, and its formula is:

$$X_c = \frac{1}{2\pi f C}$$

where f = the frequency in hertz of the AC signal, and C = the capacitance, in farads. Electrolytic capacitors are polarized, which means that they must be placed in circuits with polarity considerations.

AC Cycles

The five main forms of AC signals are sawtooth, sinusoidal, square, rectangular, and trapezoidal waveforms.

Sawtooth waveform   Sinusoidal waveform   Square waveform Rectangular wavefrom Trapazoidal waveform

There are also parts of sinewaves that are of interest.

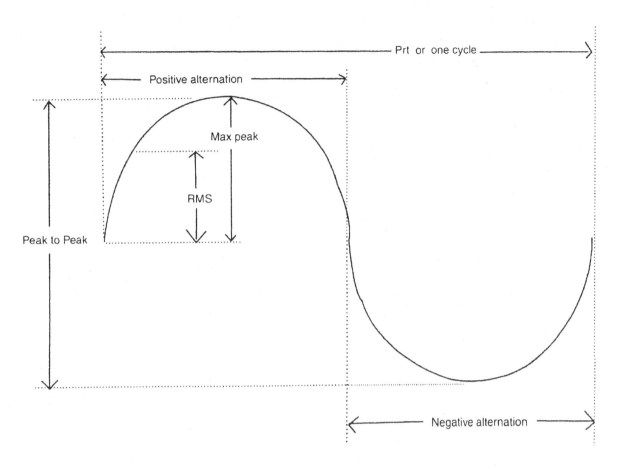

The <u>RMS value</u> (root mean square) is the same as the effective value, which is the value of an AC signal that has the same power or heating effect as a DC voltage. With sinusoidal waveforms, this value is equal to .707 times the AC voltage peak.

The <u>average value</u> is the value of an AC signal of a positive alternation and in a sinusoidal waveform is equal to .637 times the maximum voltage or peak.

<u>Magnetism</u>

The basic properties of magnetism are permeability, reluctance, and retentivity.

<u>Permeability</u> is the property of the ease with which a metal will allow magnetic lines of flux to pass through it.

<u>Reluctance</u> is a property of a metal that opposes lines of flux going through it.

<u>Retentivity</u> is the ability of a magnetized metal to stay magnetized.

Permanent magnets have high retentivity. Steel has high retentivity, low permeability, and high reluctance. Soft iron has low retentivity, high permeability, and low reluctance.

When a wire has current passing through it, the wire will have an electromagnetic field around it. The left hand rule can be used to determine the direction of the electromagnetic lines. To do this, place your left hand with fingers wrapped around the wire and your thumb pointed in the direction of current flow. The direction in which your fingers are pointing is the direction of the electromagnetic lines of flux.

Relays

The three types of relays are power relays, control relays, and sensing relays. Power relays control high voltages going to circuits such as motors. Control relays are used to energize and de-energize other relays and associated circuitry. Sensing relays are used to detect such items as over or under, current or voltages. When sensed by the sensing relay, power sources will be disconnected.

Switches

The various types of switches are identified by the number of poles, throws, and positions that they have. The number of *poles* that a switch has indicates the number of terminals through which voltages may enter the switch. The number of *throws* refers to the number of circuits that could be completed or disconnected by each blade or con- tacter. The number of *positions* indicates the number of different places that the toggle of the switch can be placed in.
The four kinds of switches are shown below.

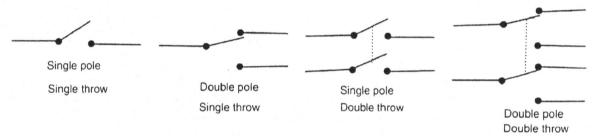

Single pole

Single throw

Double pole

Single throw

Single pole

Double throw

Double pole
Double throw

Diodes

As its name implies, a simple rectifier diode is used for signal rectification. The schematic symbol is shown below. Zener diodes are designed for specific reverse break- down voltages; and since they keep the voltage across the diode constant, they are used for voltage regulation. Tunnel diodes will give negative resistance for specific ranges of forward bias voltages. Because of this phenomenon, tunnel diodes are used as amplifi- ers or oscillators. Silicon controlled rectifiers (SCR) are triggered diodes. These are used to control AC voltages on one particular half cycle. Diacs work on both sides of the cycles of an AC signal. Triacs are gated diacs. Basically, SCRs, diacs, and triacs are used to pick out desired portions of AC signals.

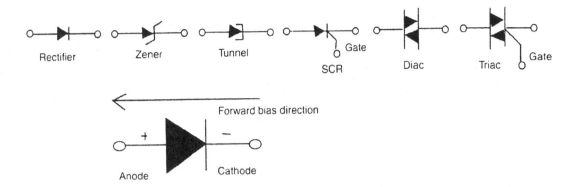

Transistors

Transistors are solid state devices that can act as amplifiers or switches. They are classified as bipolar and field-effect transistors. The bipolar transistor allows current flow in either direction. The two types of bipolar transistors are PNP and NPN transistors, which are shown below.

PNP transistor

NPN transistor

When used strictly as a switch, the PNP transistor requires a negative input signal on the base to turn it on or conduct. Conversely, the NPN transistor requires a positive signal on the base to turn it on.

Bipolar transistors are not only used as switches and have several configurations. The different transistor configurations and their respective traits are shown below:

BEG
VPI
ABG
LMH
HML
IOI

The first line is the type of configuration, i.e., common base, emitter, or collector. The particular transistor's configuration traits are shown vertically below the transistor. Line two shows electrical gains (voltage, power, or current). Line three shows the type of gain (alpha, beta, or gamma). Line four shows the input impedance of the configuration (low, medium, or high). Line five shows the output impedance (high, medium, or low).

Line <u>six</u> shows the output signal phase relationship with the input (in-phase or out-of-phase).

There are two types of field effect transistors (FET) - JFETs and MOSFETs. <u>JFETs</u> stand for junction field transistors and control large voltages with very small inputs and, therefore, can be used as amplifiers. <u>MOSFETs</u> stands for metal-oxide-semiconductor field effect transistors and have a higher input impedance and can use even smaller signals. They are also smaller and are configured by the thousands to form chips.

Soldering

Electrical connections are joined by soldering. Soldering requires a high heat source and an alloy that melts at a relatively low temperature when compared to other metals. The basic soldering technique is to first heat the joint to be soldered with a soldering device and then place the solder directly onto the joint with the soldering device still in contact. Allow the solder to melt and flow onto the joint surface covering the joint area. Once this occurs, remove solder and device, allowing to cool without any movement of the joint area. After the solder hardens, inspect the solder joint. The joint should look smooth, bright, and shiny, with the surface area of the joint smoothly covered. If the solder has the appearance of being partially balled up instead of a smooth semi-flat flow, it is called a *cold solder* joint. A possible cause of a cold solder joint might be wrongly applying the solder to the solder device and then dropping onto the area to be soldered. If the solder joint is not shiny but dull and gray instead, then the connection was probably moved prior to the solder hardening completely.

Solder is an alloy usually made up of various ratios and combinations of tin and lead. Some that are resin filled are also called flux. Soldering fluxes are used to de-oxide surfaces that are being soldered. One type of flux is acid-core resin, which is very corrosive to electrical connections and should be avoided.

Soldering devices come in various sizes, depending on the job required to be done. One of the most delicate of soldering jobs, soldering components with very small connections onto printed circuit boards, is usually done by pencil irons. These miniature irons are ideal for providing low heat to small areas. Soldering jobs that require more heat use items such as solder guns. These produce high heat and heat up very quickly.

The types of solder tips most commonly used in electrical work are made of copper or copper alloys, since copper has high heat conductivity and good tinning quality. The tinning of a soldering tip increases heat transfer/conductivity to the area to be soldered and also reduces scaling of the solder tip. Tinning consists of getting a good layer of solder on the working surface of the copper tip. Cleaning tips that become dirty or discolored requires dipping the tip in water while hot, and quickly removing it or wiping with a damp sponge or towel.

II. COMPUTERS

The 5 major components of a computer are input, storage, control unit, arithmetic and "logic unit, and output. The <u>input</u> device allows information such as data and commands or instructions to be fed into the computer system. The most common type of input device is the keyboard. Other input devices are magnetic and optical readers. <u>Storage</u> devices are used to store memory, such as instructions or data until they are needed. Memory is stored in bits, which is the most basic element of binary numbers, a 1 or 0. Bytes are groups of eight bits. A nibble is half of a byte. The <u>control unit</u> coordinates the operations of the entire computer. It interprets programs and issues instructions to accomplish the program. The <u>output</u> device communicates the progress or results of a program used in the computer to the operator/user. The devices range from monitor screens to high speed printers.

Numbering Systems

Computers and associated circuitry use several numbering systems that have different bases. We are all familiar with base 10 numbering system. This is the system we use in everyday life. In this system, each decimal/digit place represents a value of 10, whether it is the first digit to the left of the decimal point, which is a 10 to the 0 power or one's. The second digit to the left represents the number of 10's and the third represents the number of 100's.

The other base sytems work in the same fashion with their own respective bases. The other base systems used are base 2 (binary), base 8 (octal), and base 16 (hexadecimal). It is easy to convert from one system to another.

	5th digit	4th digit	3rd digit	2nd digit	1st digit
Base 10	10^4	10^3	10^2	10^1	10^0
Base 2	2^4	2^3	2^2	2^1	2^0
Base 8	8^4	8^3	8^2	8^1	8^0
Base 16	16^4	16^3	16^2	16^1	16^0

The largest number in base 10 is a 9, for base 2 it is 1, for base 8 it is 7, for base 16 it is 15. The numbers for base 16 greater than 9 are expressed by letters, i.e., 10 = A, 11 = B, 12 = C, 13 = D, 14 = E, and 15 = F.

The following is a conversion of the base 16 number to the other bases. The number will be $2B7_{16}$

$$
\begin{array}{llll}
 & & 7 & \\
2 & B^* & + & \text{Base 16} \\
\underline{\times 16} & \underline{+\ 32} & \underline{688} & \\
32 & 43 & 695 & \\
 & \times & & \\
 & \underline{\ 16\ } & & \\
 & 688 & &
\end{array}
$$

So $2B7_{16} = 695_{10}$

*B = 11

The procedure for calculating is to start with the most significant digit and multiply it by the value base used. In this case, the most significant digit is a 2 and the base value is 16. Next, take the result of the multiplication and add this to the next lower digit and then multiply by the digit place value. This was (32+11) x 16 = 688. This procedure continues until the least significant digit is reached. At this point, just add the accumulated value so far with the last digit.

This same process is used for converting any other number of a different base to base 10 number, using the respective base values.

To convert a base 10 number to its base 16 (or any base), the process is as follows: First, the base 10 number is divided by the base number of the base system it is to be converted to. To reconvert 695 base 10 back to base 16, 695/16 = 43 with a remainder of 7. The remainder (7) is the least significant digit of the new base number. Next, 43/16 = 2 with a remainder of 11. 11 is the next digit because we are going to base 16, 11 = B. Since it is less than the base number (16), 2 becomes the most significant digit. So, the converted number is 2B7 base 16.

To convert the base 10 number to base 8, 695/8 = 86 with a remainder of 7, which will be the least significant digit. Now, 86/8 = 10 with a remainder of 6, which is the next digit. Finally, 10/8 = 1 with a remainder of 2, which is the next digit. 1 is left as the most significant digit. So, 695 base 10 = 1267 base 8.

We can reverse this to see if it is correct. Multiply the most significant digit 1 by 8. 1x8=8. Add this to the next digit and multiply by 8, (8+2) x 8 = 80. Add the result to the next digit and multiply by 8, (80+6) x 8 = 688. Now, add the result to the last (least significant) digit, 688 + 7 = 695. So, 695 base 10 does = 1267 base 8.

Performing base 2 calculations is just as simple. Take 21 base 10 and convert to base 2. 21/2 = 10 with a remainder of 1, which is the least significant digit. 10/2 = 5 with a remainder of 0, which will be the next digit. 5/2= 2 with a remainder of 1, the next digit. 2/2 = 1 with a remainder of 0, the next digit. The remaining number will be the next most significant digit. So, 23 base 10 = 10101 base 2.

Reverse this to check: 1x2=2. (2+0) x 2 = 4. (4+1) x 2 = 10. (10+0) x 2 = 20. (20+1) = 21. So, 23 base 10 does equal 10101 base 2.

Flip Flops

Flip flops have one of two stable states. They change states by receiving input pulses. The reset-set flip flop (RS FF) is one of the most basic forms of flip flops made by interconnecting two NAND gates.

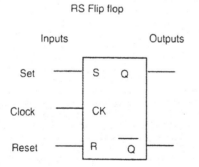

RS Flip flop

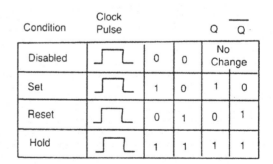

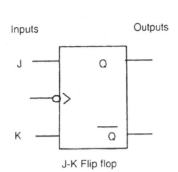

J-K Flip flop

Condition	Clock Pulse			Q	$\overline{Q}$
Hold	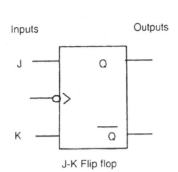	0	0	NO Change	
Set		1	0	1	0
Reset		0	1	0	1
Toggle		1	1	Change to Opposite state	

Inputs   Outputs

A flip flop with a clock input is called a synchronous device; without a clock input it is called an asynchronous device.

The most common type of flip flop is the J-K flop flip (shown on the previous page). The J + K inputs are data inputs. The arrowhead > at the clock input means that the flip flop is edge triggered. The bubble 0 means that the flip flop is negative edge triggered. Flip flops can be put together to make counters such as:

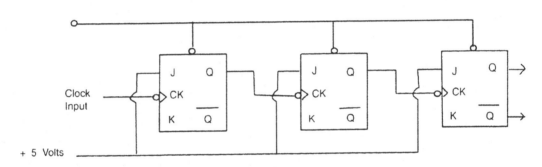

Shift registers also use flip flops in which data is loaded serially (one bit at a time). Once the FF's are loaded with data, they can be shifted left or right (depending upon how they are wired), by clock pulses. Shifting the data to the left or right will either divide by 2 or multiply by 2, depending on which FF has the least significant digit.

The following represent adders which perform arithmetic operations:

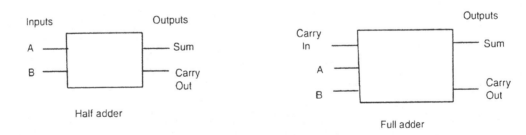

Half adder   Full adder

Half adders add binary numbers like the full adder, but do not consider previous carry inputs.

The significance of flip flops is that they can be grouped together to form units of memory, such as RAMs, ROMs, PROMs, and EPROMs. RAM (random access memory) is volatile memory, meaning that when power is turned off, the stored memory is lost. RAM is considered a read-write memory, meaning that you can read data from or write data into the memory. ROM (read-only memory) is non-volatile, meaning that when power is turned off, memory is not lost. ROMs are permanently programmed by the manufacturer and is often called firmware. PROMs (programmable read-only memory) are special ROMs designed to allow the user to program the ROM. EPROMs (erasable programmable read-only memory) are also special ROMs that allow the user to program memories and erase the programs.

Logic Gates

Logic gates use binary inputs. In positive logic, a 1 is a high input and a 0 is a low input. In negative logic, a 1 is a low input and a 0 is a high input.

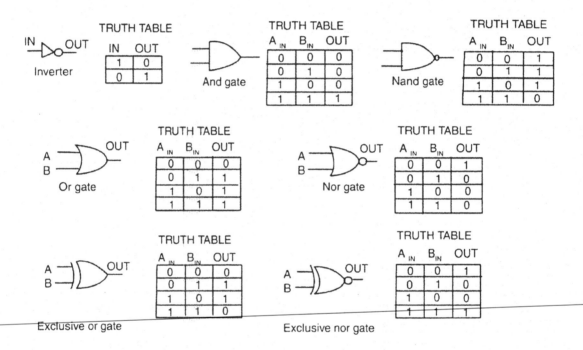

III. OSCILLOSCOPES

Oscilloscopes are used to display instantaneous voltage waveforms in graphic form. The display screen is set up and divided vertically and horizontally in 1 cm divisions. There are 8 vertical divisions in which waveform amplitude is displayed and 10 horizontal divisions in which the time of the wavelength is displayed.

The VOLTS/DIV knob allows the user to select the waveform voltage amplitude in each vertical division to be displayed. The SEC/DIV knob allows the user to select the sweep speed of the waveform in each horizontal division to be displayed.

Proper use of the oscilloscope requires the ability to analyze displayed waveforms by observing the number of divisions a cycle of a given waveform covers both vertically and horizontally.

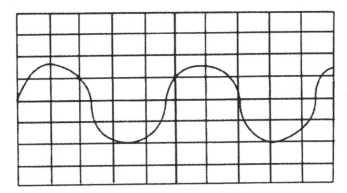

In the waveform shown above, the VOLT/DIV knob is set on 5 volts/div and the SEC/DIV knob is set to 1 msec/div.

Count the number of divisions covered vertically by the waveform, which is 3 1/2 divisions. To get the actual peak-to-peak amplitude of the sinewave, perform the following calculation: 3 1/2 divisions x 5 volts/division = 17.5 volts peak to peak.

Now count the number of divisions covered horizontally by one complete cycle of the waveform, which in this case is 4 1/2 divisions. To find the PRT (pulse repetition time), perform the following calculation: 4 1/2 divisions x .001 sec/division = .0045 seconds. .0045 seconds x msec/.001 sec = 4.5 msec for the PRT.

To find the frequency, simply invert the PRT: Frequency = 1/PRT = 1/.0045 sec = 222.22 cycles/sec or hertz.

The same process could be reversed to find the settings to use on an oscilloscope when you know the amplitude and frequency of a given waveform/signal that you would like to view on the oscilloscope.

<u>Meters</u>

The following are the basics of measuring meters: Always measure current *in series* with the circuit to be measured and always measure voltage in parallel with the circuit.

When performing resistance measurements, always ensure that the component or circuit has no voltage on it and consider whether a specific component may need to be isolated from the rest of the circuit so that the resistance measurement does not follow an alternate path. This can be accomplished by removing one of the *electrical* legs of the component from the circuit. When unsure of the amount of voltage on a circuit to be measured, start with the highest meter setting or range.

When using analog or needle deflection type meters, ensure that you have the proper polarity of leads when checking for DC voltages. One of the most popular analog type multimeters used is the Simpson 260. For copyright reasons, a copy of the meter cannot be given but here are some tips that will work using any analog multimeter. When performing DC measurements, look at the range setting that you have the meter set up for, and find the same corresponding scale on the meter face for proper readings. When performing resistance measurements, read the resistance value on the resistance scale where the needle is deflected to and then multiply this by the resistance range setting. An example of this is with the needle setting on a value of 8 on the resistance scale and the range knob on *RX1000,* then the value of resistance is 8000 ohms.

IV. SCIENTIFIC NOTATION

Scientific notation is a way of expressing large numbers. For example, 100,000,000 ohms could be written as 100×10^6 ohms or 100 megohms. Other prefixes like meg are listed below.

FACTOR	PREFIX	SYMBOL	FACTOR	PREFIX	SYMBOL
10^{12}	tera	T	10^{-2}	centi	c
10^9	giga	G	10^{-3}	milli	m
10^6	mega	M	10^{-6}	micro	μ
10^3	kilo	K	10^{-9}	nano	n
10^2	hecto	h	10^{-12}	pico	p
10^1	deka	da	10^{-15}	femto	f
10^{-1}	deci	d	10^{-18}	atto	a

V. GEARS

Gears are wheels with teeth that are used to transmit mechanical motion from one point to another. The usual configuration is that of two gears meshed together. In this configuration, the larger gear is simply called a *gear* and the smaller gear is called a *pinion.* If the pinion drives the gear, the system is called a speed reducer. If the gear drives the pinion, then the system is called a speed increaser.

When gears are used in increasing or decreasing speeds, they are configured in gear ratios. This allows specific speed changes. For example, for a gear to turn 100 revolutions per minute, if the shaft of the driving motor turns at 1000 revolutions per minute, to achieve the desired speed, it is necessary to use a reducer configuration. This is accomplished by changing the gear ratios. Since gears are made with a certain number of teeth per inch, reducing the number of teeth per inch on the gear attached to the motor shaft to one-tenth of that of the other gear that is being driven would reduce the speed of the driving shaft from 1000 revolutions per minute to 100 revolutions per minute on the driven shaft.

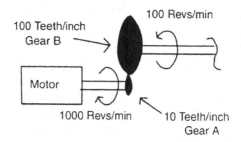

The basic formula for calculating the relationship between the gears and their respective speeds is: Revs/min(gear A) x Teeth/inch (gear A) = Revs/min(gear B) x Teeth/inch(gear B).

When two gears mesh, they turn in opposite directions. Adding a third gear called an idler gear and placing it in-between the two gears will allow them to turn in the same direction. There are four basic types of gear configurations, and they are spur, worm, helical/herringbone, and bevel gears.

Spur gears are the most common type, having straight teeth. They are used to transmit power between two parallel shafts.

TYPICAL SPUR GEAR

Worm gears having helical teeth are used to transmit power between two shafts whose axis intersect, but not in the same plane. This is probably the most common method of speed reduction, especially in conveyers because the speed of a very fast rotating motor can be greatly reduced.

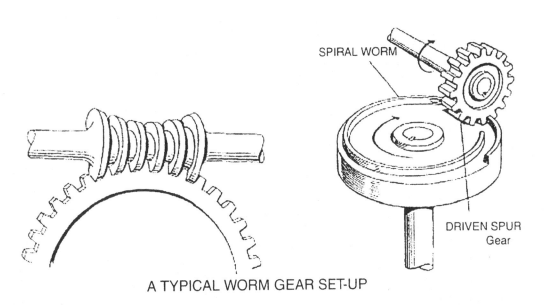

A TYPICAL WORM GEAR SET-UP

Helical/herringbone gears have spiral teeth which allows them to transmit power between two shafts at any angle.

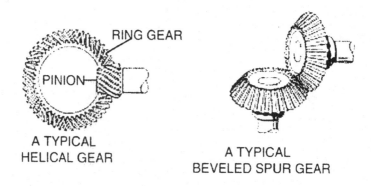

A TYPICAL
HELICAL GEAR

A TYPICAL
BEVELED SPUR GEAR

Bevel gears are shaped like sections of cones and used to transmit power between shafts whose axis intersect.

Pulleys

Pulleys are wheels used to transmit power such as pulleys used to transmit power from a motor to drive the roller of a conveyer belt. The main feature of a pulley is its ability to change speeds or revolutions per minute. When a pulley drives another pulley with a smaller diameter, the rpms of the second pulley will be greater. This results in a speed increase similar to that in gear systems.

A formula for calculating the circumference around a pulley is: $C = 2\pi r$, where r is the radius of the pulley, and $\pi = 3.14$. Through a series of derivations, the relationship of respective rpms between two connected pulleys is as follows.
Arpms = Brpms x rB/rA where:

- Arpms = revolutions per minute of pulley A
- Brpms = revolutions per minute of pulley B
- rB = radius of pulley B
- rA = radius of pulley A

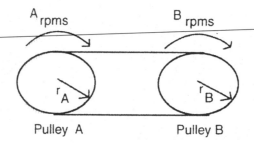

Pulley A   Pulley B

Another use of pulleys is compounding. Compound bows used for archery take advantage of the physics involved in compounding to allow archers to draw bows at high weight pulls with relative ease. For example, to pull up a 100 lb. weight, instead of having to pull with a force of 100 lbs., pulleys can be used to lessen the force required.

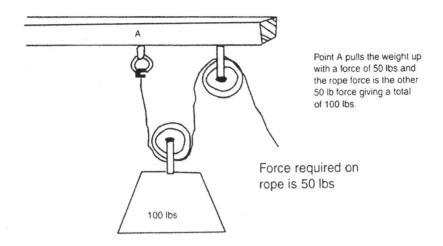

Point A pulls the weight up with a force of 50 lbs and the rope force is the other 50 lb force giving a total of 100 lbs.

Force required on rope is 50 lbs

100 lbs

A pawl is a device used to allow a wheel to turn in one direction and lock the wheel from turning in the other direction. Pawls are commonly found in winching or come-along set-ups.

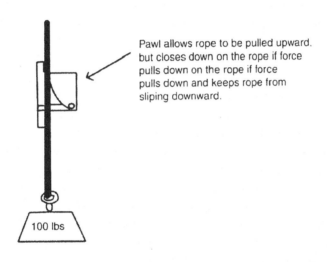

Pawl allows rope to be pulled upward, but closes down on the rope if force pulls down on the rope if force pulls down and keeps rope from sliping downward.

100 lbs

Special coupling is required in power transmissions in order to get mechanical power from one point to another. There are four general types of coupling. The first type is rigid coupling and is rarely used because the shafts must be exactly parallel and, therefore, do not allow for misalignment. The second is flexible coupling which allows for some misalignment although excessive misalignment increases wear. The third type is chain coupling which has been mostly replaced by flexible coupling which requires the most maintenance of all couplings. The last is fluid coupling which uses steel shot as a flow charge. This allows the motor to pick up loads gradually.

Chains should be mounted horizontally or not more than 60 degrees off the horizontal plane. They do allow for the most misalignment. Hook-shaped sprocket teeth show excessive wear. Misalignment may be identified by inspecting for wear on the sides of teeth on the inner surface of roller link plates. The chain sag should not be greater than 2% of the distances from the sprockets, which is 1/4 inch per foot.

A cam is a device connected to a rotating shaft used to convert rotary motion into reciprocal motion.

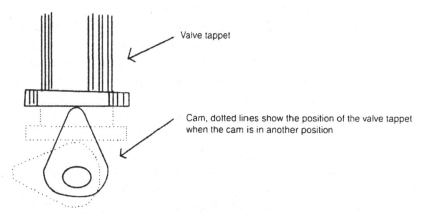

Valve tappet

Cam, dotted lines show the position of the valve tappet when the cam is in another position

Lubricants

Lubrication materials occur in many mediums. Three that will be discussed here are oils, greases, and solids.

Multigrade oils are the most versatile of the oil types. They have additives that allow them to be used in a wide range of temperatures. For example, in an oil labeled 10 w/30, 10 is the SAE viscosity number at 0 degrees Fahrenheit, and the SAE viscosity number at 210 degrees Fahrenheit is 30.

Greases are used in the lubrication of ball or idler bearing systems. Generally speaking, greases are oils that have had thickening agents or *soaps* added. The different kinds of greases are graded from 000, which is a *semi-fluid,* to 6 which is described as being very stiff or thick.

Another type of lubricant is solids. The most common type of solid lubricant is graphite. Another type is molybdenumdisulphide. Solid lubricants are extremely useful as anti-seize compounds to protect rubbing surfaces under high pressures and temperatures from metal pick-up.